On good days
I am the intrepid cameraman
in desert-crossing and jungle-hacking documentaries,
recording the other grim faces
while my own is never seen,
but I am important and ubiquitous.

On fair days
I am the breathless commentator
in desert-crossing and jungle-hacking documentaries,
wired to a studio chair
filling out the faces and the trees.
and I am as perishable as the volume knob.

On bad days
my pals have to tie my shoelaces.

Rhythm Method - Ian McMillan

FOREWORD

You know, I was never really any good at anything - or at least I thought so until 1978. True, I had had my moments at school, particularly at the primary level when George Foster and I were so ahead of everyone else that we were allowed to jump a year and sit our 11-plus examination at the grand old age of ten. George and I had also been part of the team in the Merseyside Quiz - a very prestigious event in its time. But then it had been all pretty much downhill as I ploughed my way through secondary school and tertiary education - just about keeping my head above water and keeping up with the herd as it bowled along. Certainly not showing a flair for much and definitely not excelling at anything.

And then, in 1978, in my first year in the Cayman Islands, I found myself in a race with a couple of miles to go and with a fair chance of a medal. For the first time ever I had the chance to win something through my own individual efforts. I went for it and won the bronze medal for third overall. Since that time I have never looked back and this book chronicles my running experiences in the thirty years from 1st January 1980 to 31st December 2009. Each chapter deals with a different year, the races I ran, the people I met and the things that I learned from the experience.

1980

1st January 1980

I had done a little running before arriving in the Cayman Islands in 1977 - runs under duress at St. Francis Xavier's College in Liverpool, midweek leagues at Kingston and a single run - in two years - in Jamaica, with my goalkeeper Kevin Scott - but I had never kept a proper record. Today was the day I began to do this and the record/log itself has since become a raison d'etre when and if all else failed.

Cayman running had to be done either early morning or late afternoon because of the heat and it was usually the latter, with the mosquito-spray plane in close attendance. Many was the early evening when I had to dive for cover in the undergrowth along Walkers Road.

Saturday 12th January 1980 - **Orange Bowl Marathon**

My first marathon and what an occasion it turned out to be. I had been asked to take part by someone, I think it was Tony Scott, from the Cayman Islands Athletics Federation just a couple of weeks earlier and I was not sure that I was completely ready. However my wife Mary and brother-in-law Johnny - who was staying with us at the time - urged me to have a go and so I went for it.   Frank Flowers and I, along with a couple of supporters, flew into Miami and at race registration we were treated like real international-class runners. How little they knew! On the day itself we got ready in the elite changing area alongside the likes of the great Ron Hill and we were all set to go. My main priority was to finish, secondly to enjoy the occasion and thirdly - and a distant third at that - to get a reasonable time. I certainly achieved the first two, it was a highly emotional finish and both Frank and I will never forget the reception we received and the race itself.

Splits were quite mundane: 10 miles in 69 minutes, 15 miles in 107 minutes, 20 miles in 150 minutes

Finishing Time: 3 hours 31 minutes 15 seconds
Position: 306th out of 2500

A picture of me wearing the silly red Worzel Gummage hat I wore at the time eventually ended up in my father's work newspaper back in Liverpool. Not the most photogenic of pictures by any means.

Saturday 26th January 1980 - **6th Annual Cayman Islands Road Relay**
I ran the fifth leg of the race, from Savanna to Red Bay, in 24 minutes and 21 seconds and my team, the Hash House Harriers, were first overall. This was one of a record number of times that we won the race and broke the record - something I still believe we hold today.

Saturday 5th April 1980 - **Orange County Marathon**

My second marathon, this time in sunny California. Through urban landscapes reminiscent of the film Chinatown, with much of the course being along artificial dykes and drainage canals. The weather was excellent and there was great support from an appreciative Californian crowd. The running boom was really at its zenith at this time, with all and sundry taking part. The long stretches along urban water-courses made it a little more boring than it needed to be - but I seem to remember feeling comfortable for much of the race. It was quite a low-key race in all sorts of ways.

Next day, mind you, we visited Universal Studios and my legs were constantly collapsing under me as if someone was hitting the backs of my knees. Maybe it was too soon after the Orange Bowl.

Finishing Time: 3 hours 9 minutes 57 seconds
Position: 95th out of 693

Saturday 12th July 1980 - **Grandfather Mountain Marathon**

To North Carolina for my third marathon. The race began at the Appalachian State all-weather track in Boone, North Carolina at 3230 feet asl and ended at 4279 feet asl at a Highland Games gathering at the top of Grandfather Mountain. Quite a weird event, with runners getting lifts up the mountains in cars - which meant that you were passing the same people time and time again.

When you got to the finish at the top you were given a baseball cap and that was that. No results service or other prizes. Still, the Games were good and Boone itself was an eye-opener, with corkage arrangements in restaurants and student parties at the motel we were staying at consisting of a massive tin bath full of tinnies from which we were invited to help ourselves. Apart from that, the place is bone-dry as far as alcohol is concerned.

Finishing Time: 3 hours 19 minutes 18 seconds
Position: 34th out of 204

Sunday 21st September 1980 -**Bill Rodgers Cayman Islands 10k.**
From Plantana to Lime Tree Bay. I finished in 39 minutes and 13 seconds which was a personal best and placed me 13th out of 193. The beginning of a long infatuation with this particular race. Bill Rodgers is a great chap to meet and talk with. I had the pleasure some years later to share a pre-race platform with him, advising other runners about the following day's race.

Sunday 26th October 1980 **Pirates Week Half Marathon.**
A pleasant run but in rather warm conditions. Even so I was pleased with my time of 89 minutes and 41 seconds, a personal best which placed me third overall. This race would soon switch to Saturday and I would run each year.

Sunday 21st December 1980
Saucony 'Share the Road' 10k race in Coconut Grove, Miami.

An altogether faster race than I had hithereto been accustomised to, as indeed my time showed. 35 minutes 52 seconds was a personal best by a long chalk and was hardly bettered later on. It placed me 56th out of 710 finishers.

1980 was therefore an excellent year for my running. There were races long and short, and three marathons - making me appreciate that this was indeed the event for me. Although I had not heard it at the time, Zatopek's adage was to prove to be my motivating force:

> If you want to run, then run a mile. If you want to experience another life, then run a marathon.

1980 - stats

Total Mileage for Year: 2025
Cumulative Mileage: 2025
Number of Marathons: 3
Number of Races: 9

The small number of races, the relative dominance of marathons and the contrast between weeks of high mileage (up to 70) and those of low mileage (down to 3) are all particularly noteworthy here.

1981

This was the breakthrough year in a whole variety of ways. Our first son Patrick was born - by far the key event of the year - and I dipped under three hours for the marathon for the first time, thereby qualifying for Boston. That in itself would merit a complete book.

Saturday 17th January 1981   **Orange Bowl Marathon**

The big breakthrough! First time under three hours. I knew that I had it in the bag when I spoke to another runner at 20 miles and we realised that we were on schedule to qualify for Boston with a sub-2h 50' clocking. I had a great run in exceedingly hot conditions, with two other runners from Cayman - Frank Flowers and Linda Barlow. I met Ron Hill afterwards and we drank beer in the sunshine from a tap inserted into a large Budweiser oil-tanker type truck. This really cemented my link with Miami, its palm trees, fine boulevards and acres of space. Also its balmy, sub-tropical air was a great turn-on.

Finishing Time: 2 hours 48 minutes 15 seconds
Position: 79th out of 1624

Saturday 24th January 1981
7th Annual Cayman Islands Road Relay.

Once again I ran the fifth leg of the race, this time in 23 minutes and 34 seconds and once again my team, the Hash House

Harriers, were first overall.

Saturday 7th March 1981 **Galveston Marathon**

This was rather a difficult one - up and down the Seawall
Boulevard for what seemed like forever and ever. On reflection it
was probably a little too soon after Miami and a little too close
to Boston. Several things got on my nerves, including cyclists
pacing some of the local runners. This was a slow race, with a
winning time of over 2 hours 30 minutes, as a result of a 35mph
headwind for long stretches. It also rained for this low-key race.
All was not doom and gloom however as I achieved a good
position and liked the wild, slightly weathered, nature of
Galveston. Also Texas, even Houston, was a hoot.

Finishing Time: 2 hours 52 minutes 37 seconds
Position: 12th out of 202

Monday 20th April 1981 **Boston Marathon**

Who'd have believed it? The big one. At the time this was the
most famous and most respected of all marathons. It was like
the Holy Grail of marathon running - a once-in-a-lifetime
experience. Mary was five months pregnant at the time but took
the bus to the start at Hopkinton with all of the other supporters.
This is an ideal point-to-point course with a tremendous field
assembled. I felt that I had arrived as a marathoner as I lined up
in the company of Seko and his entourage. The race itself went
like a dream, with crowds urging you on at every juncture. I felt

driven all the way in this, my biggest race so far. It would be difficult to forget even the small details like the hot stew in the underground car park of the Prudential after the race. Even today it has to be seen as the best of the lot.

Finishing Time: 2 hours 47 minutes 42 seconds   personal best
Position: 1510th out of 5074

Sunday 20th September 1981 **Bill Rodgers Cayman Islands 10k.**

I finished in 38 minutes and 54 seconds, a personal best which placed me 13th out of 205.

Saturday 21st November 1981 **4th Annual Cayman Islands Half Marathon.**

Warm to start with, but cooler later. My time was 82 minutes and 5 seconds which placed me second overall, though nearly seven minutes behind the winner.

Sunday 20th December 1981
Evian 10k Road Race in Coconut Grove, Miami.

A pleasant race which I ran in 36 minutes and 22 seconds, finishing 64th out of 748.

1981 - stats

Total Mileage for Year: 2000
Cumulative Mileage: 4025
Number of Marathons: 3
Number of Races: 8

1982

A quiet year - or was it? Only two marathons, though one of them was my first in the UK. Otherwise the year seemed to go much as any other.

Saturday 16th January 1982 **Orange Bowl Marathon**

My third attempt at this and I don't remember much about it at all. There was a larger-than-usual Cayman contingent, however, with Alan Jones, Tim Byrne and Malcolm Davies being particularly prominent. Also the previous week there had been a 10k race ('The Race of The Americas') and it was this which attracted most of the publicity. It was also very hot, despite the 7am start, and many runners dropped out. Nonetheless, Alan Jones had a marvellous race, finishing 37th overall in a time of 2 hours 33 minutes and 30 seconds. Alan was for long my nemesis and I rarely beat him - but a nicer guy you would find it hard to meet.Tim Byrne was a little way behind me and I am not sure whether Ed Wilson was there or not - though I did get the signature of Leslie Watson on my starting number and I knew that he had the hots for her. (So much so that he ran alongside her for much of the race !)

Finishing Time: 2 hours 48 minutes 33 seconds
Position: 122nd out of 1938

Saturday 30th January 1982 **8th Annual Cayman Islands Road Relay.**

My leg was the fifth again. This time my time was 23 minutes and 14 seconds and the HHH was first for the third consecutive year, establishing a new record.

Sunday 11th July 1982   **North Tyneside Marathon**

First UK marathon and what a reception we got. Three of us went over - Alan Jones, Ed Wilson and myself - and they thought to begin with that we were natives. We got a big write-up in the local press. The initial reaction was that we were top internationals and black as the ace of spades. They were wrong on both counts, of course, though they did suspect that we were perhaps schoolteachers. The liaison person was Gordon Chester - a lovely man who was great to deal with. This was quite a difficult course, starting and finishing on the links. Both Jones and Wilson, (who my father was very impressed with), beat me on this occasion - though we were sixth team and Alan Jones beat both the great Jim Alder and Harry Matthews. Their team were overall winners and they were gracious enough to share some of their prize of a case of Newcastle Brown Ale with us. Ed Wilson wrote a very amusing article about our experiences, or more precisely about the way that he set off in hot pursuit of one Leslie Watson.

Finishing Time: 2 hours 51 minutes 46 seconds
Position: 50th out of 209

Sunday 19th September 1982 **Bill Rodgers Cayman Islands 10k.**

My finishing time was 37 minutes and 33 seconds, which was a little slower than the previous year, finishing 11th out of 203.

Saturday 27th November 1982 **5th Annual Cayman Islands Half Marathon.**

Warm throughout the race and also very humid. Time was 80 minutes and 22 seconds which placed me 3rd out of 47 runners.

Sunday 12th December 1982   **Evian 10k Road Race in Coconut Grove, Miami.**

A fast race on this occasion and I was pleased to post a time of 35 minutes and 47 seconds, a personal best placing me 47th overall.

1982 stats

Total Mileage for Year: 2090
Cumulative Mileage: 6115
Number of Marathons: 2
Number of Races: 10

Some variety being introduced here but not a great deal.

1983

This was the year that I got a little over-confident about my marathon capabilities and ran a third, disastrous race at Bolton.

Saturday 22nd January 1983   **Orange Bowl Marathon**

Fourth attempt at this particular race and again I do not remember a great deal about it except that it was very warm and humid (humidity 97% at 7am; 91% at 9am) making the going very hard throughout. As with the previous year there had been a 10k race earlier on in the week and this attracted most of the publicity. My time was a personal best, however, and very close to dipping under 2 hours and 47 minutes. Also the Cayman team of myself, Malcolm Davies, Tim Byrne and Frank Flowers was 9th out of 15 in the open category.

Finishing Time: 2 hours 47 minutes 01 second
Position: 74th out of 3200

Saturday 29th January 1983 **9th Annual Cayman Islands Road Relay.**

Me on the fifth leg again and again we were victorious. My time was 23 minutes and 10 seconds, another personal best.

Sunday 24th July 1983   **Bristol Unigate Marathon**

I quite enjoyed this race, which was run in pouring rain throughout. This kept me nice and fresh . I was pleased with the whole experience in what was essentially a low-key race. I remember running around the perimeter of the British Aerospace facility at Filton - rather an uninspiring urban course but I was up for it. The race was won by Nigel Gates who went on to do some great things in Masters' running. I won a trophy (my first for a marathon) for finishing in the first fifty - a good idea I thought at the time. However, it was such a comfortable, hassle-free race that I got a little over-confident about doing another marathon later that year.

Finishing Time: 2 hours 48 minutes 6 seconds
Position: 49th out of 946

Sunday 21st August 1983 **Adidas British Marathon Bolton**
This was a mistake from start to finish. It was too close to Bristol and I was not prepared for the race at all. I was too heavy, (16 lbs above race weight), had done too little mileage in the previous weeks, had been socialising too much and was over-confident. All this in addition to an afternoon start, (so much hanging around), the warmth, the high humidity, the hills and my poor pacing - there was only one outcome, and sure enough I hit the wall at 20 miles, walked a long way and recorded a very poor time. The winner was Ian Thompson, but I knew very little about this at the time. The irony was that I got everyone involved. Even my aunt Kitty came to Bolton to collect my number, and the folks were there on the big day. But this was not a good idea, less than a month after Bristol, and I suffered

accordingly. I hope that I learned my lesson.

Finishing Time: 3 hours 17 minutes 10 seconds
Position: 508th out of 8000

Sunday 18th September 1983   **Bill Rodgers Cayman Islands 10k.**

I finished in 37 minutes and 07 seconds, a time which placed me 12th overall out of 192 runners.

Saturday 26th November 1983   **6th Annual Cayman Islands Half Marathon.**

Warm but pleasant and my time of 79 minutes and 58 seconds placed me 4th out of 46 runners

1983 - stats

Total Mileage for Year: 2161
Cumulative Mileage: 8276
Number of Marathons: 3
Number of Races: 11

No Christmas race in Florida this year but there was a little more variety, with five mile and cross country races thrown in.

1984

This was a big year, with one particularly big race, in New York, and two other impressive runs. Big event of the year, however, was the birth of our second son, Christopher.

Saturday 18th February 1984   **10th Annual Cayman Islands Road Relay.**
I did not enter the Orange Bowl Marathon this year, so this was my first race of the year. Once again I ran the fifth leg, this time in my best-ever time of 22 minutes and 24 seconds, and we won the event again, for the fifth year running.

Sunday 4th March 1984   **Mardi Gras Marathon**
This race was across the Lake Pontchartrain Causeway Bridge, the last one ever because of traffic considerations. Much depended upon the wind, which was not in our favour and meant a very boring race into a 20mph headwind. 22 miles of the race were on the bridge itself, the microphone man at the finish said that my running style resembled that of a swimmer, and I finished behind both George Kean and Tim Byrne. The sheer monotony of the race made it difficult to enjoy - an interesting idea which in reality did not amount to much. Mind you, the three of us enjoyed the city of New Orleans the previous evening.

Finishing Time: 2 hours 58 minutes 38 seconds

Position: 45th out of 517

Sunday 15th July 1984   **Bolton Abbey Country Fair Fell Race.**

This was preceded by 1 mile grass track race. In the main race I ran 22 minutes for the 3.5 miles to the water tower and back - including one section where it was necessary to wade through a river.

Sunday 16th September 1984   **Bill Rodgers Cayman Islands 10k.**

There was a big field as it was a championship race so I was pleased to be the first resident to finish. My time was 36 minutes and 28 seconds, placing me 37th overall out of 265 runners.

Sunday 30th September 1984   **Twin Cities Marathon**

This race, in Minneapolis-St.Paul, was a very enjoyable event in a great city, with gorgeous parks and brilliant weather. We had a team sponsored by Republic Airlines with the likes of Ed Wilson, Malcolm Davies Richard Peek, John Elliot, Pete Ribbins, Curtis Seymour and Paul Jobling in attendance, as well as myself and the ever-present Frank Flowers. I remember Ed and I going to Mass on the Saturday evening before the race and being asked to take up the collection. Did they know that they were entrusting church funds to a Scouse and a Scot ? Whatever, we were more than happy to oblige. Ed was a great companion on such occasions as he really relaxed and was enthused by everything - often bemused in the most pleasant of ways. He has since died and is sorely missed. There was a very strong Scandinavian element. I felt very comfortable throughout the race and recorded a personal best. Of the nine of us, five broke three hours, eight established personal bests and the team as a whole (3 to count) was 8th out of 30. A great success.

Finishing Time: 2 hours 44 minutes 09 seconds
Position: 183rd out of 4406

Sunday 28th October 1984　　　　　**New York Marathon**

The biggest one yet. When I consider how close this was to the previous marathon, I am amazed at how well I did - though it must be a lot to do with the adrenaline and the sense of occasion the event generated. We stayed with Tommy and Brigid Faranda at Croton-on-Hudson, (Jerry Harper was also there - not to everyone's liking as he headed straight for the telephone and had to be almost prised away from it), and got the train in. Jerry had his official blazer on and marched me straight to the head of the queue for my number at the exposition.

What an occasion the whole thing was. Even the International Breakfast Run from the United Nations the day before was packed with incident, with lawyers and doctors fighting over the free food at the Tavern-on-the-Green. The race itself had wall-to-wall crowds all the way. Coming over the bridge onto Fifth Avenue was an experience not to be repeated. Me, a lone runner, with crowds five or six deep on either side. Even Harlem was not so bad. Fall in Central Park was brilliant and meeting up with Mary, the boys, Tommy, (he was surprised at how well I'd done), and Brigid was a magical moment. One slightly sour note was that we missed our connection via Miami, so had to have an extra night there. I got into a bit of bother over that, but it was well worth it for the experience.

Finishing Time: 2 hours 49 minutes 46 seconds
Position: 287th out of 18365

Saturday 24th November 1984   **7th Annual Cayman Islands Half Marathon.**
Warm throughout race but pleasant enough. I always had to exert myself pretty hard pretty early to establish my position. No use leaving it until later, in my view. My time of 77 minutes and 51 seconds placed me third out of 52, Tim Byrne being the winner.

1984 - stats
Total Mileage for Year: 2082
Cumulative Mileage: 10358
Number of Marathons: 3
Number of Races: 12

A good year, with the break from racing in the summer months seeming to have worked well. New York was a great highlight, possibly the biggest event I will ever take part in. Minneapolis was by far the prettiest American city that I have ever visited.

1985

This was a breakthrough year as I recorded my fastest marathon time ever at the Florida Festival Marathon and I also ran more races than ever before, most of them in pretty good times.

Saturday 9th February 1985   **11th Annual Cayman Islands Road Relay.**
Once again my first race of the year and once again the fifth leg. My time of 21 minutes and 38 seconds was my fastest ever and the second fastest for the whole race that year. Pace was 5 minutes 24 seconds per mile which is tiring even to think about now. HHH won the race for the sixth successive year.

Sunday 17th February 1985   **Florida Festival Marathon**
This was the best one yet and turned out to be the best one ever - an all-time best result. It was a relatively low-key race and very enjoyable, with a good crowd of us at the festival. This included Chris Everett ,(who sang as he ran), Malcolm Davies and John Elliot. The race was run in a very good spirit and I enjoyed it immensely. I had changed my dietary preparations somewhat, eating fish rather than pasta in the final meal before the race. I was running well at the time and I was very relaxed. As a result I put in some good running.

Finishing Time: 2 hours 40 minutes 56 seconds   (Personal Lifetime Best)
Position: 13th out of 353

Sunday 14th July 1985   **Sandwell Marathon**

Patrick's fourth birthday. I do not remember much about this one except that my parents came along. My father went into a betting shop in Sandwell the day before the race and found he was the only white face in there. Chris Everett, immaculate in a white linen suit which made him look like the Saint, came with me into Birmingham to see if we could get some pasta. I do not remember if we were successful or not. The race started in a country park, which was nice, but much of the course was very concrete and urban. I seem to think that you could make the choice during the race as to whether you were going to do the half or the full marathon. Like most British races, as I was to discover, and very unlike American ones, there was precious little in the way of drinks and refreshments at the end. It was a very hilly course. Also running were Chris Everett, Alan Jones, John Elliot and Ed Wilson.

Finishing Time: 2 hours 47 minutes 26 seconds
Position: 18th out of 1200

Sunday 15th September 1985   **Bill Rodgers Cayman Islands 10k.**

There was a tragic loss today when Tim Butler died during the race as a result of becoming overheated. Tim was a close friend and colleague of our neighbour Alan Smith and his death was devastating for all concerned.

Saturday 21st September 1985   **Guinness/Ting Cross Country Challenge.**

I mention this race because it was my first ever solo victory in any race of any sort. I beat Tim Byrne on this morning race through the airport dykes, which I gather are there no more. I ran two more races in this series and on reflection and in the light of subsequent events, there truly was a dearth of cross-country opportunities in Cayman.

Saturday 23rd November 1985
8th Annual Cayman Islands (Washington Bank) Half Marathon

This was even better. My first time first in a major race. Beat both Malcolm Davies and Alan Jones, (though latter was coming off an injury). I was thrilled to bits with my victory and the cup. My time, 78 minutes and 5 seconds, was almost incidental. A mention here of Nick Duggan, President of Washington Bank in the islands at that time and now sadly passed away. What a fuss he made of all those taking part, what a wonderful, likeable person he was. His support for the running community was tremendous and much appreciated.

Saturday 7th December 1985   **Third CAC Cross Country Championship.**

My first international event, representing Cayman, (I still have the vest), though best forgotten in some respects as Puerto Rico murdered us. I can still envisage the whole bunch of them taking a small ridge en echelon as they swept imperiously along the course. I was 22nd out of 31, behind Alexander Brown (whatever happened to him?) and Chris Lundie.

Sunday 15th December 1985 **Channukah 10k race in North Miami Beach.**
I registered a good time here and was first in my age group. I was very impressed with the facilities in the Jewish Community Centre which served as race headquarters. Amongst other facilities they had a warm-up track inside the building on the first level - a little like an extended balcony. Ideal for inclement weather. I also ran the previous day's Jingle Bell Jog around a shopping centre - of this I remember very little, though I still have the t-shirt, as once again as on innumerable occasions it was Jerry Harper who got me there and back all in one piece.

1985 - stats

Total Mileage for Year: 2024
Cumulative Mileage: 12382
Number of Marathons: 2
Number of Races: 24

A good year, with plenty of races and two big records.

1986

Rather a lull this year, with not a great deal remembered except the disappointment of Chicago and a low key marathon in Lincoln.

Saturday 1st February 1986   **12th Annual Cayman Islands Road Relay.**

This time my fourth race of the year, after three short Saturday races from Portuguese Point. Hash won for seventh successive year. Also my house team, Wahoo, won the House Competition for the first time ever. I was on the fifth leg, of course, and ran 21 minutes and 49 seconds, giving me the fastest time for that leg and the second fastest leg overall.

Saturday 8th February 1986   **Gasparilla Distance Classic.**

Now this really was some race, over 15 kilometres in Tampa, Florida. Conditions were ideal for much of the race and my 10k time was 34 minutes and 56 seconds; final 15k time was 52 minutes and 27 seconds, a personal best over this rarely-raced distance, which placed me 145th out of a field in excess of 6000. This turned out to be one of my best-ever races at sub-marathon distance. Everything seemed to click into place on the day - a rare case of serendipity.

Sunday 13th July 1986   **Gainsborough Marathon**

This was a very rural, very small-scale race but I enjoyed the course and the general route. I stayed overnight at a pub which was very noisy and kept me awake for half the night, which did not help a great deal. This was an aspect of rural England I had not come across before, with gangs of feral young people descending on market towns and creating havoc on weekend nights - not an endearing sight. I seem to remember that Alan Jones and Chris Everett were also in attendance here. Chris and I went into Lincoln the day before the race. Mary and the boys, as well as Rita and Eugene, came to see me after the race and we all travelled back to Derby together.

Finishing Time: 2 hours 48 minutes 35 seconds
Position: 10th out of 140

Sunday 3rd August 1986   **The Derby Ten Miler.**

I remember this as it was my first attempt at the distance and one of my fastest times ever. (59 minutes and 26 seconds). Johnny, Mary and the boys gave me a lot of support at the Moor Lane Sports Centre. It goes without saying that Johnny, my brother-in-law, was always great to have around - often quite bemused though impressed and always considering new ventures. I think that this was the first time he talked about getting a van to sell faggots at events such as these. It never materialised of course.

Sunday 14th September 1986   **Bill Rodgers Cayman Islands 10k.**

I ran 37 minutes and 6 seconds - which I was pleased with as it placed me 4th overall out of 130 runners and first local runner.

Sunday 26th October 1986   **Chicago Marathon**

Or to give it its precise name, the America's Marathon. This was a big race by any standards but I did not enjoy it half as much as I did New York. It was a very urban course, hardly passing through any park areas, (remember the Twin Cities?), mainly composed of concrete surfaces with little give, and with a loop course, (2 miles was just a couple of blocks from 18 miles), which convinced me that many runners were taking short-cuts. There were also lots of underpasses - which are not generally to my liking. It was not all bad, however, as Mary came with us, we stayed at the prestigious Palmer House Hotel, where Frank Flowers sat in the lobby applying his unguents, and we had a tremendous pre-race meal at a Chinese restaurant the night before, with me being interviewed on local tv, (comparing us tucking in inside with some mad sod who was doing his last-minute preparation outside in the rain), and the waiter and us prefacing all of our orders with the pejorative 'flaming'. Among the party that night were Malcolm Davies, John Elliot, Terry Ford and Greg Rivers - a great bunch of lads of whom John Elliott is the only one I have managed to keep contact with along with his delightful wife Ann. John, incidentally, continues to run to this day, bringing a pleasant, unpressurised, straightforward approach to his running as indeed he does to his many other endeavours.

Finishing Time: 2 hours 52 minutes 9 seconds
Position: 336th out of 12000

Saturday 29th November 1986
9th Annual Cayman Islands (Washington Bank) Half Marathon

Rather a slow time of 82 minutes 15 seconds, placing me 4th out of 32, and suggesting, perhaps, that I was getting a little jaded with this and the repetition of other races also. This may well have begun with Chicago.

1986 - stats

A different sort of year but I may have begun to get fed up with the constantly recurring cycle. The following three years perhaps support this notion. The deaths of two good friends, Ferdie Goring and Charles Sinclair, in the space of less than a month was upsetting. Along with Allan (Tom) and Hilda Thompson, Benny and Jenny Moore and Ritchie and Esther Samuels they had been our best friends in Cayman and we had spent many happy hours with them - not least those idyllic Sunday afternoon's in Tom and Hilda's delightful garden right in the heart of George Town.
Apart from Gasparilla, the races I ran were disappointing. I was

very busy with the family at home and at work, and the whole pattern of the year was becoming a little too predictable for my liking. Whether I knew this at the time or articulated it in any way - well, that's another matter.

Total mileage for Year: 1780
Cumulative Mileage: 14162
Number of Marathons: 2
Number of Races: 16

1987

A complete break from marathons this year - though other events continued unabated.

Saturday 31st January 1987   **Orange Bowl 10k in Miami.**
This was run over a special course near to the cruise ship jetties. I ran 35 minutes and 59 seconds which placed me 83rd out of 1016 finishers. Of the rest, I remember little.

Saturday 28th February 1987   **13th Annual Cayman Islands Road Relay.**
First out of 19 teams, this was our eighth consecutive win. My time was 22 minutes and 35 seconds, fifth leg, and afterwards I took off with Jerry Harper for an Irish Festival in Fort Lauderdale. It cost $4 to get in and for this we saw the Clanceys, the Wolf Tones and Frank Paterson, got merry on Guinness and spent the evening dancing away at some Irish bar. Shades of Patrick a few decades later perhaps.

Sunday 26th July 1987   **Garstang Half Marathon.**
A pleasant but hilly course for this low-key race. I ran 78 minutes and 57 seconds which placed me 16th out of about 400. My mileage was very low at the time, often between 20 and 40 mpw.

Sunday 15th November 1987   **Bill Rodgers Cayman Islands 10k.**

I ran 36 minutes and 59 seconds. This placed me 4th out of 68, behind Alan Jones, Marlon Bush and Jack Wessel.

Saturday 28th November 1987
10th Annual Cayman Islands (Washington Bank) Half Marathon.

Again quite a slow time, 82 minutes and 13 seconds, which nonetheless placed me 2nd out of just 17 runners. Was there a future for the event? I certainly hoped so, if only for the effort Nick Duggan and his team put into making it happen.

Sunday 6th December 1987   **500th Hash Run.**

I mention this as the Hash House Harriers had played such a big part in my development as a runner in the Cayman Islands. From the early days with Raymond Legge, (I retain a vivid image of him setting off in the first Pirathon, as it was called then, equipped as if he was Ranulph Fiennes about to tackle the Eiger), through Malcolm Davis, Alan Jones and Richard Peek and on to Roger Yeomans at the present time, along with ever-presents like Roger Davies and John Elliott, the camaraderie and bonhomie was unequalled and the runs a great springboard to greater things. I reached the exalted position of padre/spiritual advisor - not a sort of type-casting I hope.

1987 - stats

A very low-key year. Particularly noticeable is the low mileage.

Total Mileage for Year: 1596
Cumulative Mileage: 15758
Number of Marathons: 0
Number of Races: 12

1988

Another low-key year, though it did not appear that way to begin with.

Saturday 6th February 1988   **14th Annual Cayman Islands Road Relay.**
My first race of the year, the fifth leg as usual, and we won for the ninth consecutive year. However, my time of 22 minutes and 53 seconds was only the second fastest over that particular leg, Michael Broderick, of 'Oliver' fame, beating me to it.

Saturday 20th February 1988   **Orange Bowl Marathon**
An attempt to re-acquaint myself with this great race - but an attempt which went very wrong. I lined up at the start with, among others, Liz McColgan, (I had not realised how diminuitive she was), ran for two miles, (about fifteen minutes), and then took a very nasty fall on the metal grill over the Miami River. I was badly cut and unable to continue the race. Paramedics eventually arrived and patched me up but it was a local reporter, Hector Pashell, who was covering the race for a Spanish-language magazine, who picked me up, took me back to the race start, where nobody did anything, and then took me to the hospital. Here I received 26 stitches, one for every mile I should have run. This cost $400-plus, which John Elliot kindly paid for with his card. I then rejoined Mary and the boys at the

start/finish area where we all had quite a pleasant time, all things being considered. I was extremely grateful to and kept in touch with, Hector - who, incidentally wrote an article, in Spanish, about me. I have since lost contact, much to my chagrin.

Sunday 17th July 1988   **Cambridge Half Marathon.**

We had been staying at West Runton and I thought that this would be a nice race 'nearby'. It was not that easy of course but conditions were good and the race went well. I later found that some of my future clubmates at Yarmouth in fact ran the same race. My time was 79 minutes and 21 seconds.

Sunday 9th November 1988   **Bill Rodgers Cayman Islands 10k.**

My time was 36 minutes and 53 seconds and my position was 3rd out of 41, behind Alan Jones and Johnny Miller.

Saturday 26th November 1988
11th Annual Cayman Islands (Washington International) Half Marathon

Raced well but was beaten by 5 seconds by Alan Jones. This was disappointing, though perhaps even more so was the small field of just 19. My time was 81 minutes and 0 seconds.

1988 - stats

A disappointing year from the fall in the marathon onwards.

Total Mileage for year: 1632
Cumulative Mileage: 17390
Number of Marathons: 1
Number of Races: 9

1989

A real trough. My father died suddenly during the year. He had suffered from emphysema for many years but it was still a terrible shock and of course the family would never be the same again. He knew I had resigned and we were coming home as we had regular telephone conversations. He died in May and two months later we said our farewells, packed up and left Cayman after twelve years there preceded by two years in Jamaica. There was no job to go to at the time but it was certainly time to go and at the time running took very much of a back seat.

Saturday 18th February 1989   **15th Annual Cayman Islands Road Relay.**
Groundbreaking as, after nine years in first spot, we were beaten into second place by Rivers Runners. My time of 22 minutes and 59 seconds was a little down on previous years and maybe the writing had been on the wall for a time.

Wednesday 12th July 1989   **The day we returned to England.**

Sunday 27th August 1989   **Carlton Forum 10k in Nottingham.**
Ran quite well to record 37 minutes and 32 seconds and finish 11th overall out of a field of 78. It was a little strange getting there by bus and blending in with no fuss or fanfare - quite the opposite of Cayman, of course, but something I would have to get used to now we had made the break

Saturday 30th September 1989　　　　**Diss 15, my first race in Norfolk.**

I knew no-one at the time and got the train. Finished in 90 minutes and 57 seconds which placed me 26th out of 219 finishers. I suppose I was missing the Cayman Half then.

Sunday 15th October 1989　　　　**GYRR Marine Promenade 10k.**

My first race in Yarmouth, where I now lived. Time was 36 minutes and 18 seconds which placed me quite high up in a field of 202 runners. I seem to remember finishing in the Wellesley Stadium and getting some sort of trophy from Angie Thompson - but I may be wrong. I also had run a sort of cross-country race at Bury St Edmunds the previous day, finishing 39th out of more than 80 runners. Of the event itself I have no recollection whatsoever.

Sunday 26th November 1989　　　　**Hadleigh Ten.**

A cold day and a hilly course but I think that this was fun. The time was not very spectacular though - only 61 minutes and 13 seconds.

1989 - stats

Writing about this year, (and to a lesser extent about the two previous years), has been cathartic in the sense that it has made me realise just how bogged down we were in Cayman and just how difficult it was to take the decision to leave and to bring it about. Running was way down on my list of priorities and the distances covered each week, the number of races and the overall performance are adequate testimony to this. It was time for new challenges.

Total Mileage for Year: 1358
Cumulative Mileage: 18748
Number of Marathons: 0
Number of Races: 7

My first Orange Bowl Marathon

Tight t-shirt and beanie hat

Bill Rogers race start in 1984

Happy Hashers

Sunny Days

Hash, winners for the second time, 1980.

Cayman

Teams

Mardi Gras Marathon Team, March 1984.

The Republic racers: (1-r) John Elliott, Malcolm Davies, Tim Byrne, George Kean, Mike Spragg, Frankie Flowers.

Twin Cities Marathon Team, September 1984.

MEMBERS of the Twin Cities marathon team: (from left) Ed Wilson, Paul Jobling, Richard Peek, John Elliot, Mike Spragg. Not pictured are Frank Flowers, Curtis Seymour, Malcolm Davies and Pete Ribbins.

Whitley Bay for the North Tyneside Marathon in 1982

Gordon Chester   Me   Alan Jones   Ed Wilson

New York 1984

Finishes

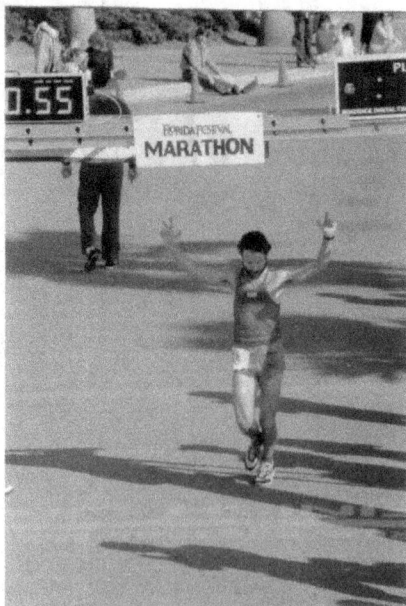

Florida Festival 1985
2 hours 40 minutes 56 seconds
My best ever

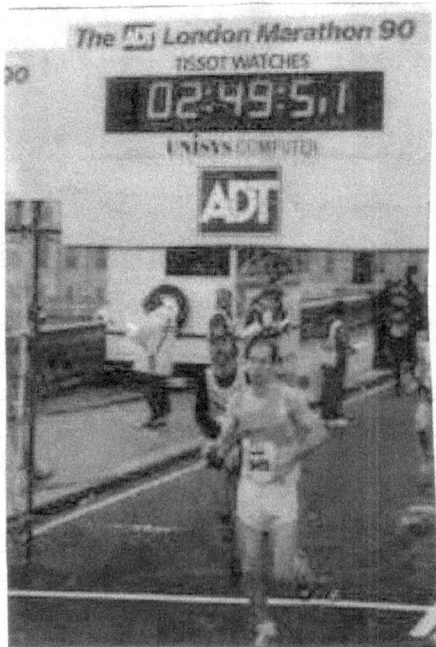

London 1990

The Caymanian COMPASS - Tuesday 26 November 1985

Page 16

Spragg runs away with Washington Bank Half Marathon

Veteran marathoner Mike Spragg literally ran away from the field on Saturday and raced to an easy victory in the third renewal of the Washington Bank and Trust Inter-national Half Marathon road race.

The bearded campaigner was hardly pressed in scoring his first major victory on the local circuit as he completed the 13.1 miles course in one hour, 18 minutes, five seconds—almost five minutes ahead of his nearest rival, fellow marathoner Malcolm Davies, who ran 1.23.02.

Alan Jones, another veteran, came along to capture third. He clocked 1.23.28.

Running in pleasant conditions, Spragg was able to take the race in a slower time than that which gave him third place last year.

In 1984, Tim Byrne, winner of the first two runnings, ran a record 1.14.45 and Spragg finished at 1.17.51. Byrne was unable to try for a third straight win as he was off the island.

As expected, Herfa Ebanks was the dominant female in the field and her 15th place finish was good enough for first place among the ladies. She didn't have an easy time of it though as Charlotte Clarke came next, just 13 seconds slower.

Again, the winning time were far off last year's. Herfa ran 1.39.56 compared to her best run last year of 1.32.59.

But this was a slower race all around. The field

Washington Bank Half Marathon

My biggest victory in Cayman Half Marathon Winner

Spragg

Final times

Name	Time
(1)Mike Spragg	1.18.05
(2)Malcolm Davies	1.23.02
(3)Alan Jones	1.23.28
(4)John LaFrance	1.23.43
(5)Ed Wilson	1.27.52
(6)Tim Hayes	1.28.29
(7)Pete Ribbins	1.30.45
(8)Jim Fraser	1.31.33
(9)Reg Koster	1.32.59
(10)Hesmer Hydes	1.34.09
(11)Peter Stafford	1.36.34
(12)James Davidson	1.37.26
(13)Marc Powell	1.39.34
(14)Martyn Bould	1.39.48
(15)Herfa Ebanks	1.39.56
(16)Charlotte Clarke	1.40.09
(17)Tom Taylor	1.41.08
(18)Allen Bloomrosen	1.42.42
(19)Clarence Flowers	1.42.48
(20)Gregory Rivers	1.43.13
(21)Terry Ford	1.44.18
(22)Conrad Cacho	1.54.24
(23)Gary Caswell	1.56.43
(24)Sandra Wellington	1.56.59
(25)Mandy Basham	1.57.19
(26)Graham Basham	1.57.20
(27)Sherree Ramsay	2.01.13
(28)Herb Cohen	2.02.11
(29)Mark Ford	2.10.22
(30)Tony Scott	2.16.35

Race Finishes
and handovers

FINAL hand over from Mike Spragg to Ed Wilson
for HHH and the race is almost won.

ATLETA BRITANICO SE ACCIDENTO

Para Michael Spragg, maratonista británico, quien viajó desde Islas Caymán para participar en el maratón que forma parte de "The Orange Bowl Running Series" celebrado el 20 de febrero, lo que debió ser una fiesta deportiva se convirtió en frustrante experiencia.

Durante las primeras millas del recorrido de 26.5 millas Spragg sufrió una aparatosa caída cuando pasaba por el puente de Brickell Avenue, causándose varias heridas de consideración.

Nuestro reportero gráfico, Héctor Pashell, se encontraba en el lugar del accidente cubriendo la prueba para AFICION, y al notar que el corredor no era auxiliado y que las voluntarias más cercanas ignoraron lo ocurrido, se dirigió a un oficial de policía para solicitar la presencia de los para-médicos, los que se limitaron a cubrir las heridas de Spragg y se marcharon.

Inmediatamente nuestro reportero trasladó al atleta al puesto de socorro, donde le prestaron los primeros auxilios y sugirieron que el herido fuese trasladado a un hospital. Lamentablemente, por la falta de previsión de los organizadores de la competencia, no se contaba con ninguna ambulancia o vehículo disponible para tal propósito. Nuestro reportero, en gesto que se debemos destacar, llevó al herido a un centro hospitalario del área donde le fueron suturadas las heridas.

Esperamos sinceramente que este lamentable incidente sirva para que se instruya a los voluntarios que son localizados a lo largo del recorrido, sobre qué hacer en casos de accidentes como el ocurrido a Michael Spragg, y así como para mejorar el sistema de primeros auxilios en las competencias venideras.   A.P.

Hector Pashell's account of my accident

1990

Patterns of the past years had gone and it was now time to see how England matched up as far as running and races were concerned. The year started very slowly - 4.5 miles in the first week! - I know not why, but things then seem to have got better.

Sunday 21st January 1990   **Beccles Ten Miler.**

A very disappointing run for me as I was beaten by both Ken Overy and Dick Norman. My time was 64 minutes and 34 seconds. Ken and Dick, incidentally, along with Len Gooch, were instrumental in helping make the transition to running in the UK so smooth and even pleasurable - such was their friendliness and willingness to let me get involved in the heart of things.

Sunday 25th February 1990   **Bury 20 Road Race.**

A race I did not enjoy as it was windy, quite hilly and consisting of a number of dreary underpasses. Not what I was used to at all. Time was 2 hours 12 minutes and 26 seconds. I was well and truly beaten by Ken Overy here. Ken, a lovely man, still exudes a warm glow when he speaks of this race, possibly his finest ever performance with a time which remains a club record to this day and is unlikely to be broken in the near future.

Sunday 11th March 1990   **Little Plumpstead Hospital 10k.**

A very pleasant course this, though only my third 10k since returning to the UK. I remember seeing if I could get Paul a job at what looked like a nice hospital. Not much luck in that respect, however. Time in race 37 minutes and 30 seconds.

I then ran half marathons at Diss in March and Bungay in April. These were in preparation for the big one, the London Marathon.

Sunday 22nd April 1990   **ADT London Marathon**

The big one after a few months back in England. Travelled to London with Dick Norman - a wonderful companion - and stayed at the Sherlock Holmes Hotel on Baker Street. A long walk to the Pasta Reale party in the evening took quite a bit out of us. I did not enjoy the starting arrangements at Greenwich, especially as it was cold and damp to begin with, but the race itself went pretty well and I was pleased with my time. Also met up with John Elliot - who had a tough time of it - and went for a drink afterwards. Also I was beginning to make my presence felt on the local running scene as this was a big group from the Athletics Club - including Mike Smith and Angie Thompson. Overall, I did not like the London event, however, and was never tempted to do it again. I always felt, and increasingly so as the years have passed, that the organisers acted as if they were doing you a favour letting you take part - rather than the other way around. If you like, a Ryanair sort of approach, as opposed to a Eurostar one.

Finishing Time: 2 hours 49 minutes 56 seconds
Position: 1121 out of 26000 finishers.

Sunday 17th June 1990   **Norwich Half Marathon.**

This was the first of many and I enjoyed it immensely. It started from Chapelfield Gardens and had an interesting course. My finishing time was 1 hour 19 minutes and 20 seconds.

The rest of the year saw 10ks at Burnham Thorpe, Lowestoft (twice) and Yarmouth - in two of which I dipped under 36 minutes for the first time in this country. In the second of the Lowestoft races I beat Gary Zupan, a rare occurrence, as a result of an unusual bit of basic psychology - entirely coincidental. In very warm conditions and with about two kilometres to run, I was ahead of him by a metre or so and offered him a drink of water. He indicated that he would like some but could not speed up to such an extent as to draw level with me. I therefore knew that I had him and beat him at the end. Gary, incidentally, a keen competitor, moved back to South Africa some years later.

Sunday 9th September 1990 **Great Yarmouth Seaside Half Marathon.**

Another pleasant race, finishing on the track at the Wellesley Sports Ground. My time of 1 hour 17 minutes and 40 seconds was very pleasing.

Sunday 30th September 1990　　　　　**Thunder Lane Five in Norwich.**

This was a stinker of a race with two laps incorporating the notorious hill of that name. I am still surprised at my time of 29 minutes and 15 seconds, placing me 10th out of 91.

1990 - stats

The year ended with the Turkey Trot at Lowestoft and this and other races were the first signs of a new pattern which was to emerge in the UK. I was pleased with my London time and the variety of races I ran.

Total Mileage for Year:　1697
Cumulative Mileage: 20445
Number of Marathons: 1
Number of Races: 14

1991

As the number of races proliferates, it makes no sense to itemise them one by one, except in the case of marathons and other races of particular significance. I will therefore confine myself to listing the races to begin with, before selecting some of note and then discussing the particular marathon in detail.

This year saw races at Beccles, (still a pb at 59'18"), Bungay, Rotterdam, Peterborough, Lowestoft, Newcastle, Yarmouth and Stalham. Although there seems to have been a dearth of races, and my log was a little bare and disjointed, three races stand out especially.

Sunday 12th May 1991   **The Great East Run at Peterborough.**
Sponsored by Zanussi and with a strong field, (including some top Kenyans), I was very pleased with the outcome of this as I ran a personal best of 1 hour 15 minutes and 50 seconds, running strongly throughout and beating Richard Polley on the run-in. It seems unlikely that I will better this time.

Sunday 15th September 1991   **The Great North Run at Newcastle.**
Another top run - with thousands in attendance. I stayed with Brian Kitchener at a very nice country club at Yarm, a very pleasant spot. There was a whole busload of Road Runners in attendance but I did not know many of them very well. Micky

Munt kept everyone amused on the coach up to the north-east. The dual start, (with Ken Overy trying a fast one), meeting Eamonn Martin at the finish, and Eddie Craze puking out of the minibus as we made our exit, these are all memories I retain of this particular day. I also nearly beat Dale Hurren on the long run-in to my time of 1 hour 19 minutes and 8 seconds. Although I believe that I beat him in one of the Wymondham Summer Ten Milers some years later, this was about as near as I got to matching Dale, a likeable adversary who continues to run well to this day.

Sunday 21st April 1991   **Rotterdam Marathon**

This was an excellent race, one of the most enjoyable yet. The start and finish were both right in the city in a large building where runners were allocated a floor where there were showers, changing and massage facilities. The course was fast, very scenic and passed through many parks. I stayed in a small hotel in Feyenoord where you could have anything you wanted, (and most people did). The crowd at breakfast in the morning sort of gave the game away. There were some very attractive young ladies plying their trade in that establishment.

Finishing Time: 2 hours 47 minutes 47 seconds
Position: 338th out of 12500

So 1991 was not noted for the number of races but for the quality of three in particular. They were all great experiences.

1991 - stats

Total Mileage for Year: 1887

Cumulative Mileage: 22332

Number of Marathons: 1

Number of Races: 8

1992

A racing year dominated by the fact that, unusually, I ran two marathons, in Barcelona and on Merseyside, enjoying both of them in the process. There were also the usual races at Bungay, Stalham, St. Neots, Lowestoft (twice). I also got injured with torn muscles in the ligaments of the calf in September which meant a big reduction in weekly mileage (fourteen miles in two weeks) and missing the Robin Hood Marathon at the end of the month.

Sunday 15th March 1992　　　　**Barcelona Marathon**

This was a beautiful marathon, using the Olympic course which was to be used three months later for the big event itself. We were taken out by scenic train to Mataro and then ran back into the city and up to the stadium. Only Montjuic Hill presented problems as the last two miles were just one uphill struggle. It was well worth it to finish in the stadium, however. Crowds were exceptionally supportive, shouting 'Brava' all the way round. Mary also gave me a lot of support on this one, even though I got lost after leaving the stadium at the end and she was left holding a quite heavy bag for quite some time. We stayed at the Hotel Lloret where we had a very enjoyable Saturday afternoon. I remember it vividly.

Finishing Time: 2 hours 48 minutes 56 seconds
Position: 216th out of 5694

Sunday 21st June 1992   **Mersey Marathon**

I had not intended to do this as it was so close to the Barcelona race but I was glad I did it in the end. It was a joy to do my hometown marathon - me who struggled to run a single six-minute mile when at school - and to finish so highly placed that even Paul, often begrudging in his praise of certain things, was impressed. It was also fortuitous as the event has since been discontinued and replaced by a half marathon. (A similar thing happened in the case of the Norfolk Marathon some years later.) I was particularly pleased to be able to run this one for Vinnie Green, who was dying of cancer. We raised over £1000 to send him to Lourdes and I got to meet him before he died. The Knights of St. Columba organised the sponsorship as I have always been against it, not feeling it right to ask people for a share of their well-earned money. The race itself consisted of two loops, (not ideal), including long stretches along the prom at Otterspool and through Sefton Park. My brother Paul looked after Patrick and got up to all sorts of escapades with him. My aunt Kitty was away and let me borrow the mini - which broke down at the top of Penny Lane.

Finishing Time: 2 hours 48 minutes 39 seconds
Position: 19th out of 490

1992 - stats

Total Mileage for Year: 1839
Cumulative Mileage: 24171
Number of Marathons: 2
Number of Races: 7

1993

Just one marathon this year, and not a very distinguished performance in that, but plenty of other races at places such as Sudbury, Diss, Southport, Kings Lynn, Derby, Stockholm, Framlingham, Geldeston, Bungay and Lowestoft. On reflection this turned out to be the most diverse running year so far if you consider the range of locations. There were also two firsts - the Round Norfolk Relay and the cross country race on Outney Common, Bungay.

Saturday 5th June 1993   **Stockholm Marathon**

This was a long way to go on my own. A beautiful setting with most of the race run through parkland and along the water's edge. But the city was expensive and a bit too clean for my liking. A little like I found Norway some years later. For some reason I always much preferred Denmark and Finland to the other two - which I felt should be run by happier, more fun-loving people like the Australians or the Kiwis or the Brazilians. I did stay at a great hotel, the Globo Arena, a very modern edifice where major sporting and music events are held. I also met Hugh Jones, previous winner of London and some other major marathons and still quite close to his peak at that time. I tried to inveigle my way onto the bus for the elite runners by attaching myself to Hugh's coat-tails but they were having none of it. A far cry from being in the elite area with Frank Flowers in Miami all those years ago.

This was a Saturday afternoon race run in very hot conditions. I liked neither as there was a long time waiting around and getting hotter. I was going well until 30k but then I hit the wall big time and just struggled home in under three hours. Stockholm itself seemed dull after all this and I am not sure I made the most of it - though I did recall the Gamla Stan underground railway station in a quiz recently.

Finishing Time: 2 hours 59 minutes 22 seconds
Position: 332nd out of 8170

Sunday 19th September 1993
Round Norfolk Relay Leg 13 from Geldeston to Schole, a distance of 19.83 miles.
I ran at 1.30 in the morning - not something I would recommend - accompanied by Dick Norman on the bike. This was the only race ever where I had to put on clothes as the run progressed and I got colder and colder. However, with the help and encouragement of Dick I enjoyed the outing tremendously, and my time of 2 hours 6 minutes and 29 seconds - a pace of 6 minutes and 23 seconds per mile - went someway to offset my poor performance in the Bury 20 some years earlier.

The Great Yarmouth Road Runners team was 6th out of 16 teams.

Sunday 12th December 1993
The Annual Bungay Black Dog Cross-country on Outney Common -

my first cross-country event since returning to the UK four years previously - and it showed as I had no idea about pace, footing, line to take and so on. As a result I was in the mud more than out of it and beaten comprehensively by both Chris Hogg and Dick Norman. It did, however, stir in me a great love for cross-country which I retain to this day, preferring it to any other sort of physical activity bar none. It has given me so much pleasure over the years and I have always sought to promote and encourage it.

1993 - stats

Total Mileage for Year: 1771
Cumulative Mileage: 25942
Number of Marathons: 1
Number of Races: 10

1994

The year's racing started early with the Eastern Counties Cross Country Championships at Essex University in Colchester, in the company of eight others, including the mighty Martin Piggot. Then on to the roads at Thetford, Paris, Norwich, Mildenhall, Lowestoft, the Round Norfolk Relay, (Smeeth to Kings Lynn - Leg 2 at the time - getting a little lost as we approached the finish at Lynn Sport), and finally rounding it off with another cross country, this time at Fritton. So only eight races in all - and not a 10k among them - but perhaps partly explained by the fact that I did lots of refereeing this year (Christopher being 10 years-old, so at sort of a peak in this regard), though this seemed to help with using different muscles and employing short bursts of speed - something I still try to do in my races.

Sunday 24th April 1994   **Paris Marathon**

This was without doubt one of the best. The start on the Champs Elysees was magnificent. I stayed in a small hotel-cum-brothel the night before, (seems to have been a bit of a pattern after Rotterdam), went to a special runners' Mass on the morning of the race, jumped in very close to the elite runners at the start and went on to have an excellent race. The day before I had seen the sights from the metro - on the day itself I saw them again during the race. There was not a dull moment in this one. It continued my love affair with France and the French - first kindled thirty years earlier - in 1964 - when, en route to Saumur - I had heard a Frenchman intoning the Notre Pere in Notre Dame. I have adored Paris ever since and this trip simply confirmed my love for the place. Consider my pre-race day in Paris. I took the metro to Trocadero (registration); then Notre Dame for lunch; Porte Champeret for the hotel; Champ de Mars for the pasta meal and then to bed. What a brilliant day. A father and son playing accordion on the metro was just one small addition to an excellent experience.

Finishing Time: 2 hours 50 minutes 08 seconds
Position: 544th out of 15939

Apart from the races, one other thing which happened this year was that I started to introduce pyramids, parlauf and the like into my training, with what I believe were very beneficial results. Two cross-countries were also pleasing but not the fact that there were only eight races.

1994 - stats

Total Mileage for Year: 1806
Cumulative Mileage: 27748
Number of Marathons: 1
Number of Races: 8

1995

A rather undistinguished January characterised by low mileage and poor weather was sort of resurrected at the end of the month at the Southern Counties Cross Country Championships at Parliament Hill, scene of some of my best races while at Kingston. Three laps of three miles each in muddy conditions represented the most enjoyable cross-country yet for me. There was nothing in February but early March saw the Fenland Half Marathon at Wisbech where I recorded one of my slowest times ever over the distance (1 hour 22 minutes). Much better was the Saturday of the same week when I ran the National Cross Country Championships in Luton and was second Yarmouth runner to finish, behind Derek Gathercole. As we were leaving, I still recall Derek telling us to wait, wait, wait until the remaining t-shirts were practically given away. What business acumen that man has! Then in April I did my first race in the Great Yarmouth Five-mile Series and was pleased with my sub-thirty minutes time.

Sunday 23rd April 1995   **Turin Marathon**

I flew into Milan on the Thursday before the race. It was very lonely without Mary and after the fun we had had in places like Barcelona. I met a very nice Italian man called Mario Salmona on the plane and he seemed to think that Milan was a dangerous place for such a sensitive soul as me (smile) so he got me settled at my hotel, the Hotel Andreola. I must appear very naive and helpless on such occasions but I keep reminding myself that I am from Liverpool and the school of hard-knocks. Didn't see a blade of grass until I was six, that sort of thing. The following day I took the train to Turin, (remembering, as we left Milan station, the time my brother Paul was expelled in that very place for throwing a sweet wrapper out of the train window), and went to the race headquarters which was just over the road from the station. There I met Anna Christina of the race directorate, a nice lady who saw me to my hotel, (there you go again), and made sure that I was settled in at the Hotel Roma. The pasta party in the rain the evening before the race was attended by the racing driver Fernando Alesi and after that I went to Mass.

The race itself was point-to-point so we were taken by train out to the start in the foothills of the Italian Alps at Avigliana. We then ran back into Turin. Simple as that - except that it absolutely poured down for much of the race. Nevertheless it was a particularly pleasant course, especially those sections along the banks of the River Po. I was pleased with my time and enjoyed being in Italy and among the Italians. I could well understand why my Father loved Italy, (and particularly Perugia), so much. This was one of the most welcoming marathons of all.

Finishing Time: 2 hours 52 minutes 56 seconds
Position: 287th out of 2075
Age category: 22nd out of 272

Later on in the year I ran the City of Norwich Half Marathon - a minute down on my time of the previous year - and races at Gorleston, (the one-off John Franklin 10k), Mutford, (where I met Nicola and Colin from Cayman and had a nice chat), Wissey for the half marathon there, another one-off in the form of the Cross-Suffolk Road Relay, (my leg from Yaxley to Stortford Heath), Mousehold for the Cross-country league, and the Norfolk Cross Country Championships at Fritton Woods, (I was beginning to like this cross-country business) - these races brought the year to a close, a year which was completely overshadowed by the tragic deaths of my brother Paul in March, (a shining light extinguished), and my brother-in-law Johnny in November, (here's to you my ramblin' boy) - events which left everyone numb and from which we will never truly recover. My running exploits seemed then and seem now very insignificant in the grand scheme of things. Johnny had encouraged me to have a go at my first marathon, the Orange Bowl of 1980 - after following me on the bike around South Church Street in George Town on Grand Cayman - while Paul had always been interested in my exploits and had given me a lot of support during the Mersey Marathon. I loved them both dearly.

1995 - stats

Total Mileage for Year: 1745

Cumulative Mileage: 29493

Number of Marathons: 1

Number of races: 12

1996

I got right into things this year with a cross-country league race at Lyng near Dereham in the very first week. This was followed by nothing until the February race in the same league, this time at Fritton where we were the first veterans' team home. A week later there was the Eastern Counties Cross Country Championships at Earlham Park, Norwich, where Herbie Hide received his never-to-be-forgotten instructions to run where he liked. The fourth cross-country race of the season, and the biggest yet, was the Southern Counties' at Luton - which was very hard going indeed. Hard and rutted surfaces did the back no good at all.

So the first road race of the season was not until 17th March, the Wymondham Ten, where I ran well and dipped under 61 minutes. I missed a scheduled half marathon at Lowestoft two weeks later, mainly because I was in a choir performance at the time, and so the next big event was my annual marathon.

Sunday 14th April 1996   **Vienna City Marathon**

This was one of my least enjoyable marathons for a number of reasons. To begin with I did not find the Austrians very welcoming - the woman in the hotel, for instance, was not very helpful at all. The city itself I found cold and austere. The pre-race get-together was interesting as it took place in the main town hall, the Wiener Rathaus, and consisted not of pasta but of Austrian torte - tasty but not ideal for a pre-race meal. Memorable also were the burly american footballers holding us puny runners back at the start in what were very cold, snowy conditions. I ran a very badly-paced race, losing it completely in the Vienna Woods and having to walk from the 38 kilometre mark onwards. I had gone out too quickly - 30k in 1 hour 58 minutes and 11 seconds - and paid the price later as I passed in and out of consciousness, eating and drinking all that was given to me. This was my worst marathon yet - certainly on a par with Bolton in 1982. The only (slightly) good point was that I did manage to revive somewhat in the last kilometre, which enabled me to just dip under three hours. Overall this was, however, a race best forgotten. The snow throughout the race was the least of my worries.

Finishing Time: 2 hours 59 minutes 11 seconds
Position: 11th out of 291 in M50 category. Also in top 10% overall - always a desirable target.

The rest of the year saw races at Yarmouth, Dereham, Norwich, (where I dipped under 1 hour 20 minutes for the half marathon), Hadleigh, (for the relays), Gorleston, Holkham, Norwich again - this time for the inaugural running of the Lord Mayor's 5k City Centre Classic - a real balls-breaker as I referred to it at the time, as you had to go flat out all the way for fear of being yanked out of the race at the half-way stage. Nice to do once but no thank you again. Being there for the first running of an event also made a change from being there for the last running, as referred to previously.

In late July I was in the East Coast Half Marathon at Great Yarmouth and then a bit of a hiatus before the Grunty Fen Half Marathon in September, where I was first male vet 45-49. The year was then wrapped up with cross-country at Sheringham in November and at the Norfolk County AAAs Championships at Earlham Park in December where we were the third vets team, (me, Mike Collins, John Bone, Gary Stanley and Ken Overy). All in all this had been an interesting year, marked early on and later by cold, snowy conditions but eventful in the middle. I had also exceeded 2000 miles for the first time since 1985.

1996 - stats

Total mileage for year: 2003
Cumulative Mileage: 31496
Number of Marathons: 1
Number of Races: 17

1997

Again the year started with the Lyng cross-country and that bloody great hill which even Martin Piggot was impressed by. Then there was the February cross-country at Frettenham - so the familiar pattern of racing was beginning to emerge. We were at Luton on 1st March for the Southern Counties Vets' Cross Country where Derek Gathercole did his famous waiting, and waiting, and waiting, game before jumping in and getting a whole batch of t-shirts for next to nothing.

The first road race of the year was a 10k at Saxmundham where I set a new club record in the over 50 category. This was turning out to be a very quiet year for racing as the next race to appear was my annual marathon.

Sunday 13th April   **Antwerp Marathon**

This proved to be a very under-rated race in a very under-rated place. I ended up enjoying it immensely which I suppose goes to show that the least you expect, the more likely you are to be pleasantly surprised. It was incredibly low-key. Registration took place from 6pm the evening before the race. Roads were cleared and barriers erected just a couple of hours before the start. It was a truly city centre out-and-back course. I ran comfortably throughout and was very pleased with my time. There was good food and beer and I really came to appreciate fully Belgium and the Belgians. This was something I was to build on later with my field trips to Brussels. Antwerp itself had a lot to offer, with its zoo opposite the railway station, its diamond quarter, the River Scheldt, (nice run along it), and other aspects, perhaps a little sleazy but nonetheless attractive in their own way. Jane and Mike McLeman were there with me and ran the 10k.

Finishing Time: 2 hours 52 minutes 26 seconds
Position: no idea

After the marathon the number of road races attempted increased quite noticeably. There were further 10ks at Stalham in May and Peterborough in June; Ten Milers at Dereham in May, Wymondham in June, Barnack near Cambridge in October and the Turkey Trot at Lowestoft in December. Apart from the Barnack race, these were events which I would continue on a year-by-year basis - but only if I felt that there was a specific need. It is good to test yourself against previous performances and other runners; but unwise to repeat events blindly as this can lead to stagnation and even atrophy. For this reason I was constantly searching for new events, new experiences. One such was the Fitness Five at Barnham Broom in June, (John O'Leary's first race). Another was a five mile race from Greshams School in North Norfolk. In the other races we were consistently well placed for vets team prizes (with Ken Overy, myself and Martin

Rudrum forming a team with a combined age of 150 - being 60, 50 and 40 respectively), and I was dipping below 30 minutes for five miles, close to 60 minutes for ten and close to 36 minutes for 10k. Movement was unfortunately to be away from such marks rather than closer to them in subsequent years. The Wroxham 5k in September was a new venture and I dipped under 18 minutes and quite enjoyed the experience. The year ended much as it had begun. Not much mileage but a couple of good cross-country races, including the first in the East Anglian Cross Country League, which was to become the mainstay of our running at the East Norfolk Sixth Form College in future years. We enjoyed the cornish pasties and tea afterwards. I rounded off the cross-country year in style at the County Championships at Bawsey Park where we got the silver medal as second vets team.

1997 - stats

Total Mileage for Year: 2021
Cumulative Mileage: 33517
Number of Marathons: 1
Number of Races: 20

1998

An interesting year, this, as there were two marathons - each of them significant for different reasons. Before that there was the usual round of races at cross-country, beginning once again at Lyng in January, and on the roads, beginning at Wisbech in March. I also ran the first of many races in the Ryston series, having been talked into it by Gary Thurtle and Luke Blackwell at the college. Those guys were so enthusiastic, Gary in particular. The midweek league was also becoming a regular feature and I was putting in some reasonable performances there. I also ran the rare distance of 15 miles in the Broadland 15 and was pleased to finish 5th overall in a time of 1 hour 33 minutes 09 seconds. We then had a lovely Easter in Rome and then there was the Breckland 10k which was also the County Championships. I was disappointed with my time which was just over 37 minutes, my slowest for some time.

Sunday 24th May 1998   **Prague International Marathon**
For once I came unstuck in my travel and accommodation arrangements. Arriving late in the city I found that there was just nowhere suitable to stay. Many tram rides after my early evening arrival I found myself in a sort-of bombed-out building with no reception, no facilities, in a shared apartment with two English guys who I never actually got to meet. I barricaded myself in my

room and vowed that I would never again fail to pre-book - or, at the very least, make sure that I went with somebody else. Prague itself, however, was delightful, (if a little over-run by Germans, who seemed to be buying up everything they could lay their hands on), and the race went very well. I met Mike Gratton - but the biggest thrill of all was that the race was started by my hero, Emil Zatopek - in my view the greatest long-distance runner ever. I tried to see if he was still around at the finish but no such luck. He has since died so this really was a missed opportunity. I ran comfortably and felt pretty good throughout the race, ending up third in my age category.

Finishing Time: 2 hours 51 minutes 55 seconds
Position: 121st out of 2222   Age category: 3rd

The middle of the year saw me fall and bruise a couple of ribs - which made running difficult, (I did not run for two weeks), - and then there were the usual summer races, including the Mutford Relays, the Worstead Five, (first in my age category but just pipped by Mick Collins), the Wayland 10k and the East Coast Half marathon, where I ran well and won county gold. In late August Monsignor John Meaney, our pastor in Cayman, and some friends of his visited us and then in early September I attempted my second marathon of the year. There is an interesting story as to why I decided to run this one.

Sunday 6th September   **Wissey Marathon**

This was an unexpected surprise as I had not particularly planned to run, feeling that one marathon a year was quite enough thank you. However, the previous year at the same race, when I had run the half, I had noticed the rather pedestrian pace at which the marathon field set off. I thought, therefore, that I would give it a go. I was also mindful of the fact that Gary Zupan from the club had won the event with consummate ease on a previous occasion. The race went very smoothly and I ran most of the way, (up to 23 miles), with Kevin Vaughan of St. Edmunds Pacers - much faster than me but less experienced over the marathon distance. I managed to shake him off in the final few miles and finished second overall in the race, behind a chap from Yorkshire who was a long way ahead, and ahead of his club-mate from Yorkshire, who had also been well ahead of me but took a wrong turning towards the end. This mistake fortunately did not make any difference to the fact that I was Norfolk Marathon Champion for the first time, (not just an age-category winner), and in this, the last marathon to be run in Norfolk - at least for the time being. A great honour and a wonderful surprise. Kevin Vaughan remains a friend to this day.

Finishing Time: 2 hours 50 minutes 45 seconds
Position: 2nd of 41

The rest of the year was perhaps a bit of an anti-climax, but there was the Round Norfolk Relay after a break of some years,

(I ran from Wells to Salthouse on this occasion), more cross country at Bacton, Sheringham, UEA, (when the tragic death of Mike Groves was announced and I ran like fury), and Barnham Common. The year was rounded off with the novelty Red Lion Relay from the pub of that name down by the river in Norwich. The end of a pretty eventful year, with races at a whole range of distances, with nearly a half of them being cross-country. Teams of ten or more were regularly going to the midweek league and the weekend Norfolk League from both the club and the college. And to cap it all I was the Norfolk Marathon Champion at a time when you had to run the specific event to win it - rather than the system which replaced it - that is the postal marathon where times are submitted from races run far and wide. (I continued to win that too for a few more years.)

1998 - stats

Total Mileage for Year: 1980
Cumulative Mileage: 35497
Number of Marathons: 2
Number of Races: 23

1999

This was the year that I started to run championship races over the marathon distance, beginning with the World Veterans' Championships in Gateshead in August. Before that, the year's racing followed a familiar pattern. There were cross-country races at Lyng, Barnham Common, (Norfolk Championships, where we were second vets team), Bury, Yarmouth, (on the beach), Fritton Woods, Marsham Heath, Mousehold Heath, (where we clinched the Norfolk League title by just one point from Norwich Road Runners, much to the chagrin of Mick Powell), and finally Shouldham Warren, where we brought the midweek series to a very satisfactory close with Martin Piggot and Mike Collins both winning their age categories, Matthew Moore getting the First Junior award and me finishing second in my age category. The same week it was back to the roads.

This began with the Wymondham Ten, where we won the team prize. There was then another cross-country race, the BVAF National Championships, held that year in Norwich, which attracted the likes of Harry Matthews. In other words, a very high standard indeed. I was 31st out of 47, which sort of puts things in perspective. Mind you, we had a good session with all the lads in the Fat Cat afterwards.

Back on the roads there were the Lowestoft Half along the front and the coast road, (since discontinued) where I was 4th out of 100 - though I felt that my time was on the slow side, (1 hour and 21 minutes), and I was beginning to think of personal worsts rather than personal bests. Then the Breckland 10k, where we won the vets team prize and I won my age division - many £s worth of vouchers, not to be repeated in subsequent years, despite, or perhaps because of, our expectations. The end of May saw a disappointing run in the Ipswich Jaffa Ten but I bounced back a little in June at the Norwich Half, where I ran a better time than Lowestoft and we were the winning vets team. I now began my preparation for the marathon in August, increasing the mileage and having the occasional race - such as the Mutford Relays, (1st in age division). Then it was off to Gateshead.

Sunday 8th August 1999   **World Veterans' Marathon, Gateshead**

My first championship event. This was a great occasion, with Martin Piggot and John Bone. We all drove up to Gateshead, (295 miles), and stayed at a hotel opposite the Metro Centre. I didn't really like either the hotel or the access to it but the organisation at the stadium was great. Met Bob Sexton and John Barwick and watched many of the other events in the stadium. I was a little disappointed that the start and finish were not in the stadium itself but on the road outside. I ran well, in spite of some adverse comments about my surging from fellow Brits in the early stages. There was also a bit of a nasty hill at the end as we came up from the river bank. I ran a fair part of the two-lap course with a local lass, ('Sheila'), and an Irish chap whose name I didn't catch - though I got the impression he was a former champion of one sort or another. There was quite a bit of concrete along the course, especially on the far side of the river, but generally it was good - especially on the Newcastle side. Martin Piggot ran brilliantly and won gold, thereby becoming world champion, in his age division. He was 5th overall in the whole race, in a time of 2 hours 32 minutes 46 seconds. What a competitor he is. He brings the same high degree of professionalism and organisation to all his endeavours. You certainly know it when you are up against him in a race. I was 12th over 50, placing me 58th overall. John Bone was 20th over 50, placing him 88th overall. An excellent performance all round. It was nice to have Mary and the boys there too, as they saw me in at the end - though once again it was a pity that it was not in the stadium itself. Mustn't grumble, though, as it was the World Championships after all. We then went up to Scotland and over to Ireland to complete a very interesting holiday.

Finishing Time: 2 hours 52 minutes 40 seconds
Position: 58th   Age Category Position: 12th

The rest of the year was generally low-key, though there was my first Lowestoft Scores race, a great favourite of Gary Stanley's, the Round Norfolk Relay, (Leg 12 from Schole to Thetford - 17.77 miles), the resumption of the midweek cross-country league at Shouldham Warren and then Bacton, followed by the first running of the Hereward Relay from Peterborough to Ely. This is particularly worthy of note as we had the winning team of Gary Stanley, Martin Piggot, Mike Collins and yours truly. I ran the final leg and held on in the face of a very strong headwind, (I rationalised that it was the same for everybody), and a closing runner. I beat him to the railway crossing and from then on I knew that I had it in the bag. Even so it was a difficult race over a multi-terrrain course, (so which shoes to wear?), and I cannot say that I particularly enjoyed it or looked forward to tackling another. We were first overall out of 69 teams and it was great to bring the lads home without letting them down. The final races of the year were at UEA and Barnham in the midweek league, (the latter the one where the start was missed by Martin, Mike Collins and Jeff Helmore - much to their embarassment, though they did manage to resurrect the situation due to a particularly amenable race director) and then we were off to the Holy Land for the Millenium. Over half the year's races were now cross country, an interesting development and a very reassuring one.

1999 - stats

Total Mileage for Year: 2017

Cumulative Mileage: 37514

Number of Marathons: 1

Number of Races: 23

2000

The year began with our return from our once-in-a-lifetime visit to the Holy Land where I did not run at all, for three reasons - firstly, there were very few suitable places, (though I did consider the campus of the university), secondly it was risky and dangerous to be running about for no apparent reason; and thirdly, and most important, it did not seem appropriate to do so in such holy places where our sole purpose for being there was a spiritual one.

Back home it took a little while to get into the swing of things - though there was the Norfolk County Cross Country Championships at Quiddenham near Thetford where we won the veterans' team prize in spite of a very negligible contribution on my part, finishing well behind Martin Piggot, Mike Collins and Jeff Helmore. Nothing else in January, but February saw cross country races at Barnham Camp and Yarmouth beach which soon got me into the swing of things. Then from the word go in March there were races at Fritton Woods, RAF Halton in Buckinghamshire, (the South of England Veterans' Championships - I went down to the event with Pat Brightman), Bury and Shouldham Warren in the midweek league.

After seven cross country races, my first road race of the year was at Southport on Good Friday. I had run this race before, but on this occasion Mary and Mother came along too. An enjoyable race but my third slowest time ever over the 10k distance. The Breckland 10k a week later was a lot better, (close to 37 minutes), and then there were races at the Norfolk Showground, (an Ekiden event), and the Norwich Half, (where we won the vets, team prize but Martin Piggot had to withdraw injured). It was then off to Finland.

Sunday 16th July 2000   **European Veterans' Marathon, Finland**

My second championship event. I was beginning to take a liking to these. Two negatives to begin with were that I had to get back earlier than the others as I was still at work; and Martin Piggot had been injured at Norwich a few weeks before so could not take part - though he did accompany us even so, flying out on the Saturday and taking an interesting train journey north from Helsinki to Jyvaskyla. All four of us, (myself, Martin Piggot, John Bone and Jeff Helmore), were very impressed with Finland - its people, its trains, its cleanliness, its level of organisation. Our accommodation was not marvellous as there had been some mix-up over the booking. We had an interesting evening before the race trying to find some milk during a thunderstorm. Martin had an interesting encounter with a very drunk Finn, the two of them apparently understanding one another in a language which seemed to be something akin to Rab C. Nesbitt Scottish. I was the first of the three of us to finish but I did not find the three-lap course to be particularly to my liking - especially the concrete sections and the long hauls on the overpasses/underpasses. On reflection, my time sort of tells the story as I only just got under three hours - I could see the clock as I entered the sort of u-shaped finishing area outside the magnificent sportshall, (again there was no stadium finish, however - always a great pity in my view). Despite having to get back for work on the Monday, which took a little shine off the experience, I enjoyed my trip back to Helsinki in the upstairs section of the double-decker train which I more or less had to myself, (plus waiter service and free drinks - British train travellers could only dream of this), and thoroughly enjoyed this wonderful Scandinavian country.

Finishing Time: 2 hours 59 minutes 22 seconds
Position: 11th over 50   My fourth slowest marathon ever

It was quite a low-key year after this, though I did the 5k at Wroxham in late August, but nothing in September and then the Felixstowe Half Marathon in October where, despite running my second slowest time ever over the distance, I ran comfortably, enjoyed the race and picked up an award in the process. There was then a 10k at Martlesham Heath in the company of Mike Collins and then by November we were back at cross-country in the form of races at Bacton Woods, (always a favourite of mine), Sheringham, (in the company of Derek Ribbands), UEA Colney, (muddy but enjoyable), and Yarmouth Dunes, where a pleasant run was had by all and I beat Jeff Helmore for the first time for quite a while over the country. Interspersed with all this was our second attempt at the Hereward Relay, which we had won the previous year, a venture which was far from being as successful as previously. A larger field, drawn from a wider area and with much better runners, left us a miserable 18th out of 91 teams. I ran the leg from Whittlesey to March, but only enjoyed it in sections. The year ended with the Red Lion Relay on December 26th, 17 teams of 4, decided on the day and with plenty of beer afterwards. There had not been the range of races this year, (no ten-miler, for instance), and this may have had an effect on my overall performance.

2001 - stats

Total Mileage for Year: 2007
Cumulative Mileage: 39521
Number of Marathons: 1
Number of Races: 21

Start of Great East Half Marathon, 1991.

● Out in front. Giovanni Rizzo leads from the start. . .and was never headed. (Photo: GER5/5).

My fastest Half Marathon

Battling it out in an early cross country
at Bawsey

Start of an early Wymondham Ten Mile race.
Soon to be swallowed up by pack.

OFF: Some of the competitors get under way in the successful Wissey Valley Races.

Start of Wissey Marathon, 1998
My biggest victory in Norfolk
Norfolk Marathon Champion

European Silver at Potsdam, 2002

With Jerry Harper, my guru, in Cayman in 2002

With the legendary Ron Hill, one of my inspirations,
at Rivington Pike at Easter 2003

Yarmouth Teams

Ken Overy (40), Martyn Rudrum (40), Me (50) in 1996

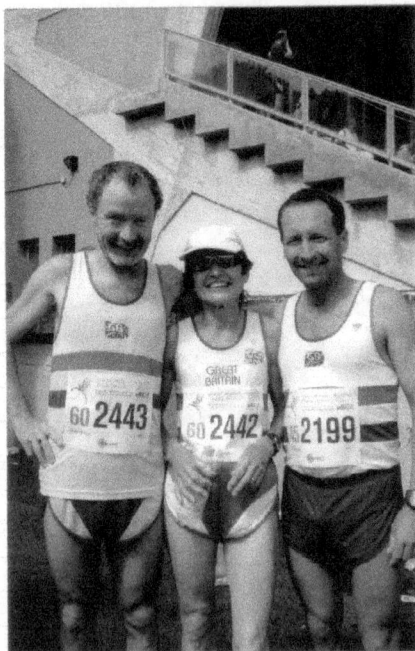

Me, Carole Spong and Jeff Helmore in Riccione in 2007

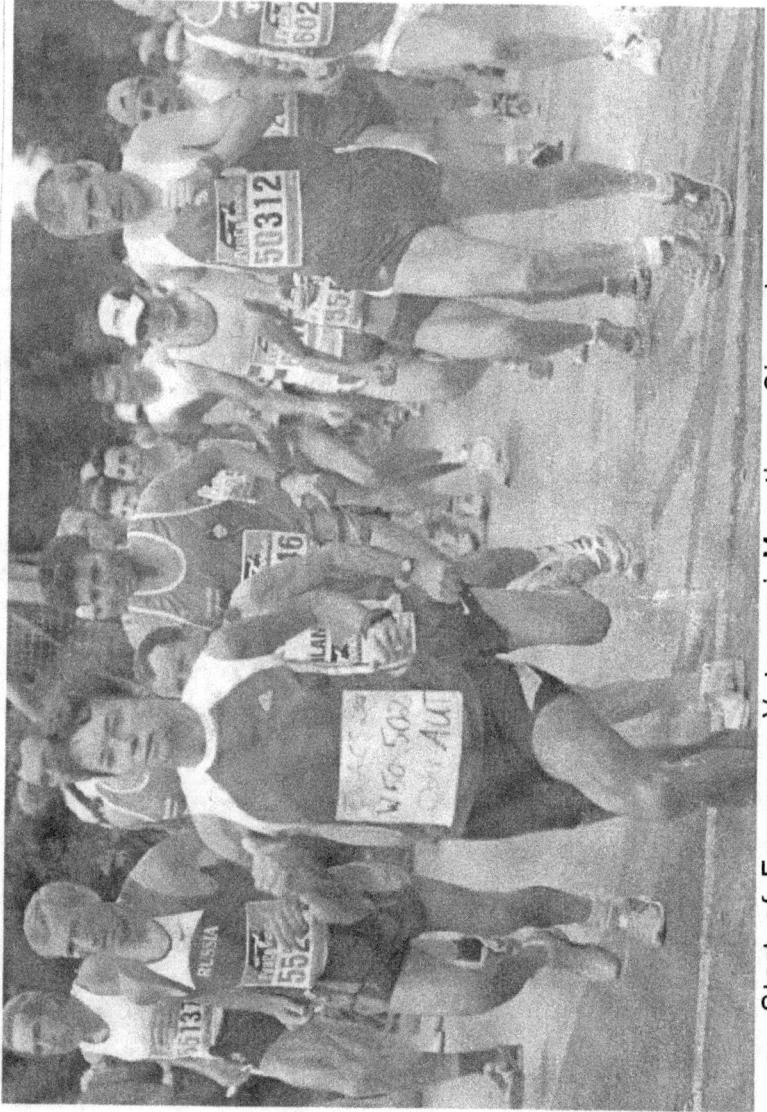

Start of European Veterans' Marathon, Slovenia

My final marathon, August 2008

One of last cross-country races of 2009

Richard Blake   Me   Neil Sibley

2001

A very unusual year, this, as, for the first time since 1989 and only the third time since I had started running, there was no marathon to take my fancy. Perhaps it was the fact that I was now totally hooked on championship events and there were none within my range that year, (there was Brisbane for the World Vets but that was a little too far), and maybe I was a little disappointed with my time in Finland - though I did not give it a great deal of thought at the time. Whatever the reasons, this was to be a year of half rather than full marathons - with quite a lot of non-running activities taking place besides.

The year began predictably enough with the Norfolk Cross Country Championships at Earlham Park where Mike Collins, Jeff Helmore, Chris Harbord and myself placed third. Then the midweek league at Bury, a very wet and cold Norfolk League race with Mike Collins at Mousehold , another midweek race at Stow Country Park, wherever that is, and the final race in the midweek series at RAF Marham, where the subsequent series' prize-giving was most disappointing as they seemed to make it up as they were going along.

This after a long and arduous season for most of those

concerned. My first road race of the season did not take place until the 25th of April, the first race in the Yarmouth Five-mile series where I ran quite well but still outside thirty minutes. Race 2 in May was 12 seconds slower and I did not do the third race for some reason. I did however throw in the Stalham 10k on the May Bank Holiday and was second over 50 on this occasion. A return to normality came with the Norwich Half Marathon in June, where I was very disappointed with my time and only third position in my age division - but we did win the team prize. I also felt that I had been particularly weak in the last couple of miles.

In the same month I did a mens' 5k at Wymondham in what I thought was a slow time - though it got me third place and I had run 13 miles the previous day, or so my diary informs me. Within the week I was at it again over 5k, this time in the Wroxham event where Martin Stacey, Richard Blake and myself won the team prize. I still found it very much a struggle, however, over this shorter distance.

Early July saw the Mutford Relays and July was rounded off with the Worstead Festival Five Mile Race, ably organised by my old mate Terry Quigley, where I was pleased with my time as my leg was troubling me for some reason.

We were then off to China, would you believe? Beijing, Wuhan,

Three Gorges, Chongqing - what an experience. I ran in the crowded streets whenever possible and was amazed at how many people there were out and about at what, to us, would be ridiculously early hours of the day. They were doing their Tai-Chi, their aerobics, their work-outs on the swings and roundabouts. Young and old, rich and poor, professionals and artisans. An old man who must have been ninety if he was a day was on the swings, not pushing a grandchild but keeping his own body in trim. Everyone was more than willing to talk and to let me join in. What an experience - the rickety and positively dangerous old treadmill on the ship was certainly no substitute for this. The only negative of the whole, relatively short, trip (just 8 days), was the food - which we sort of held up with for the first four days or so but later got what must have been dysentry for the second half of our trip.

Certainly I was still having difficulties over a week after our return when we were in the middle of our next great venture of the year, that is Patrick's play at the Edinburgh Festival Fringe. Again what a week! The whole occasion was tremendous. I find the Scots hard to get on with and some of Patrick's friends were, like many young people, very self-centred, but the whole week was brilliant and I was a little sorry that I had entered the following Sunday's Great Scottish Run in Glasgow. Having spent a fair part of the previous week on the bog and trying to get my guts right, I did not expect to run well - and so it proved.

I was very sluggish for much of the race and only perked up in the last five miles or so. Running up Arthur's seat, (pardon), on two occasions in the previous week had clearly done me no good whatever. I ended up recording one of my slowest times ever for the half marathon distance - 1 hour 25 minutes and 03 seconds. Still 6 minutes and 30 seconds per mile, however, which I suppose would translate reasonably well to a decent time for the full marathon. Glaswegian reaction to runners in general and marathoners in particular seemed similar to that manifested by Scousers, (and I'm sure Dubliners too), - a slight air of bemusement put perfectly happy to put up with such activities so long as they do not interfere with the really important day's matters, whether it be getting to the shops or to the pub.

The rest of the year saw the Lowestoft Scores race, where we fielded a strong team, (I was only our fourth finisher), the Round Norfolk Relay where I thoroughly enjoyed the 15-mile first leg which I ran at a pace of 6 minutes 43 seconds per mile from Kings Lynn to Hunstanton, and then into cross-country again in November. Although I had run it before, this was my first major foray into the Ryston Series, at the instigation of Luke Blackwell and Gary Thurtle - both of whom hoped to beat me. (Gary called me an old man on one occasion - anathema !)) I was thrilled to run the 9k course in record time, beating my old adversary Bert Wilkinson in the process. With the Hereward Relay in late November and the midweek league in Fritton Woods the same week, (when I beat several good people), a strange run organised by North Norfolk Beach Runners in Cromer Happy Valley, (too hard and too dry - part of it along the seawall), and the next race in the Ryston Runners' series - this time over the 6.5k distance where I again broke the record, the year drew to a reasonably satisfactory close.

2001 - stats

Total Mileage for Year: 2000
Cumulative Mileage: 41521
Number of Marathons: 0
Number of Races: 21

2002

This was to prove to be the most successful year yet as far as my marathons were concerned as, quite out of the blue, I got the European silver medal in my age group in Potsdam. This was a great honour and I was thoroughly overwhelmed to achieve it. It made all the times and miles put in worthwhile.

The year began not with the Norfolk Championships, which I think were cancelled for some reason, but with the fourth Ryston race, where I again broke the course record - this time over the short course I then got a foot infection which meant a week off, but I managed the Beccles Ten after this and was tenth overall. Then there was more cross country at Yarmouth and Ryston again, then the St. Peter's Brewery 20k, a very friendly race in which I finished 20th. We were then in Shannon for the funeral of Monsignor Meaney and after this there was the midweek cross country at the UEA and the Wymondham 10 in the same week - rather a disappointing time in the latter, perilously close to 63 minutes. March saw the final Ryston race, where I again broke the record, this time my own, and was disappointed not to get the overall series prize for best runner - I certainly felt that I deserved it. This was the beginning of a slight ambivalence in my feelings towards the Ryston club. I then missed the Broadland 15 because of a cold but was ok for the Bungay Half in April, where I put up with the long, seemingly never-ending hill from Bungay to Beccles and finished 13th out of over 325 in a quite respectable time for this difficult course. I was certainly a lot faster than my time for the Great Scottish Run.

Mary's mother died in April and after our return from the funeral I was putting in some very good (for me) weekly distances - regularly getting quite close to sixty miles a week. The key, I think, was the Tuesday and Thursday sessions where I needed to cover 25 miles in total, as Saturdays could be adjusted accordingly.

May saw my tenth race of the year in the form of the Breckland 10k, where I was third in my age group, then the Dereham Ten where I struggled in the latter stages of what I regard as a boring race, but still set a new club record over the distance, winning my age division and the vets team prize into the bargain.

Another club record was set in June's Norwich Half where I had a much improved time on the previous year and felt comfortable throughout, perhaps, I noted, because running the day before, (I did 8.6 miles), seems to help. The Wroxham 5k about ten days later was altogether quite draining, though I felt that I did well at my pace, which was 5 minutes 54 seconds per mile. The Wymondham Ten (fourth to Mark Hudspith) rounded off June in fine fashion. I had an exciting race in early July with Richard

Blake when I just held him off in the run-in at the Ryston Midsummer Five Series - where we both dipped under thirty minutes and, along with Gary Thurtle, got an unusual little clock trophy for our efforts. Again I had set a new club record. Mileage was good for the rest of July and I managed to do a little, (25 miles), in our visit to Poland. Straight back and I ran the first two races in the Norwich Midweek Series - the 5k - and the 10k - where I again ran well. I was then all geared up for Potsdam.

Sunday 25th August 2002 **European Veterans Marathon   Potsdam**
This has got to be the culmination of my marathon running career. It may well have been the time to call it a day on this particular distance. I don't know. Certainly in many respects it was the best of the lot. Jeff Helmore accompanied me and we flew from Norwich to Amsterdam to Berlin. We had a great day sightseeing the day before, stayed at a glorious hotel complex, the Seminaris, Jeff was a great travelling companion, and the race itself went like a dream. My 10k splits were fine for the first 20k and only just went over the 40 minute barrier for the second 20k. One of my isotonic bottles went missing but the other two served their purpose well. I was exhilirated at my finishing time, which placed me second Briton overall, (all ages), and, more importantly, as I was to discover later when called to the podium in the middle of a quiet drink outside with Jeff, second in my age category, (out of 90 runners), sandwiched between two Russians. It was so unexpected that I had to borrow a shirt from

the British team manager in order to step up on the podium and receive the silver medal and flowers from none other than Jorgen Busch, the Olympic silver medallist in Mexico City. What a great, wonderful and unexpected honour - it certainly made me feel very proud. When the certificates were being written up I got a great round of applause from a group of American competitors and their wives, likewise when I got back to College. I offered up the silver medal for my wonderful mate Bryn Pike who had died so suddenly earlier on in the month on the 12th August.

Finishing Time: 2 hours 54 minutes 17 seconds

Position: 45th out of 497 males   2nd over 55 out of 90+   2nd Brit overall

That same week I did the Wroxham 5k, to ensure victory in the Grand Prix, and there followed races in the Round Norfolk Relay, (again Kings Lynn to Hunstanton), Ryston, (age division and course record over the short course), Bacton, Honington (twice) in the midweek league, the Hereward Relay, Ryston twice more - and that was it for the year as we set off for Cayman and I managed a run with the Hash from Roger Davies' house on December 30th. What a year.

2002 - stats

Total Mileage for Year: 2291

Cumulative Mileage: 43812

Number of Marathons: 1

Number of Races: 28

2003

This was a year when I did not intend to do a marathon, I did one, had a torrid time of it, but still recorded a very satisfactory time. The year began much as usual with cross-country races at Ryston and Hadleigh in January, (the latter being an amazingly difficult race with cold winds, a hill twice and the most cloying mud imaginable). February saw more cross-country, this time at Nowton Park in Bury, and the St. Peter's Brewery 20k race at Bungay, where I was first over 50. Right at the beginning of March was the Wymondham Ten Miles, followed in that month by the final Ryston Race, (a new course record over the 6.5k distance). After not much in early April, I ran the Rivington Pike Fell Race on 19th April (Easter Saturday). With the benefit of hindsight I probably should not have done this as I had some bad muscle problems later on in the week, being hardly able to walk. However, I did get to meet Ron Hill again and have my picture taken with him, I did not disgrace myself and I was not far away from winning one of a number of very generous prizes. There was 777 feet of ascent, for heaven's sake! - so a time of 24 minutes and 9 seconds was not at all bad. I was second vet over 55 and 74th in a field of 219. What a great man Ron is. Still running every day, ticking off the countries and miles, (though he now talks in terms of kilometers), and retaining a refreshing and straightforward attitude to the sport he loves, (hearing his views on pacemakers in big city marathons is a treat in itself).

The Breckland 10k in May saw one of my slowest times ever over the distance, (38 minutes 06 seconds), and this was followed by races at Leeds, (the half marathon where I had an excellent race to finish second over 50 and win a kit voucher. This was an excellent, well-organised race which made full use of the city centre. I went with John Hills), Dereham, (again faster than Wymondham but not as enjoyable), and the Norwich half in mid-June, which doubled as the British Vets Championships and where I finished third in the over 55 age group. I notice that through all this time I was regularly doing a long Saturday run to either Berney Arms or Burgh Castle - something I somehow found difficult to repeat the following year. In late June I was second in the county ten miles at Wymondham, (behind Pete Johnson), and in July it was the Mutford Relays. In August I was second to Richard Blake at the run-in at the Norwich Midweek 10k, though pleased with my time, and then we were off cruising, where I saw my first glacier up close and got used to regular 10k sessions on the treadmill. I then managed the Wroxham 5k and the Lowestoft Scores in the same week, but in September I was only the non-running team captain for the Round Norfolk Relay. I did, however, turn out for the Equinox Five at Lowestoft, where I was first over 50 and just dipped under thirty minutes. Then came my thirty fourth marathon, a race I had never intended to run until urged to do so by the visiting Dutchman, Ton Rojmein, and by the fact that I heard that John Elliot and his boys were to be there.

Sunday 19th October 2003   **Amsterdam Marathon**

I am still not sure that I should have done this one. I got talked into it by Ton Rojmein. In the end I probably ran better than I should have - though my mileage had been good up to that point. I had trained right through the summer and reached 60 miles a week on occasions, also I had a few decent races under my belt. It was a bit messy getting a hotel after flying out with Mary from Norwich, and I wasn't that pleased with where we ended up, (too far out of the centre). This was a big race with certainly in excess of 10000 runners. Start and finish were in the 1912 Olympic Stadium, (where we also ran through at 7k), and so, with Mary, Ton and John around, what could possibly go wrong? Well plenty in fact. The course was a loop with one nasty, long out-and-back section along one of the major canals - which seemed to go on and on. The first 10k went very well (39'41") and I got very confident at 20k (1h18'33") and 30k (1h 58'52"), passing people left, right and centre - and surging as if I was in a 10k event. I really paid for all this foolishness at 32k onwards, however, when I more or less lost it - almost unable to run at times, disoriented and almost losing the will to go on. Certainly I was half hoping to be over 3 hours as this would give me a plausible reason to give the event up. As it was, when I did eventually enter the stadium in a very bedraggled, half-dead fashion, I was amazed to discover that my time was quite respectable and indeed on a par with that of Potsdam over 12 months previously. I was also fourth in my age category, something I found out as I crossed the line as the Dutch, in their usual efficient, organised way were giving out bunches of what looked like lilies to the first three finishers in each age category - and the Belgian who just beat me was just a few metres ahead.

So the hard effort early on had paid off in the end. Even so I hope never to have to experience the likes of that final 10k again. As a postscript, neither TJ nor JE and his boys were to be seen at the end, though Mary did buy me a lovely drink.

Finishing Time: 2 hours 54 minutes 56 seconds
Position: 168th out of 3535 4th over 55 out of 164
(Behind an Italian, a Finn and a Belgian)

Straight after the marathon was the first Bacton cross-country, then Ryston, (new course record), Barnham and a new series at Mousehold Heath, Norwich. Also races at UEA and the Great Barford Half. The year ended with a resounding thud when my poor Mother died on 16th December after a number of extremely miserable years when her physical and mental faculties declined alarmingly.

2003 - stats

Total Mileage for Year: 2107

Cumulative Mileage: 45919

Number of Marathons: 1

Number of Races: 25

2004

The year began with the Norfolk Cross Country on January 4th at Earlham Park, and the rest of January was to follow a familiar pattern with cross-country races at Ryston, Mousehold and Yarmouth Dunes, the latter an East Anglian Cross Country League race which was exceedingly cold and snowy - though I did beat both Jeff Helmore and Richard Blake, so it cannot all have been bad. I was training with Nola Turner at the time, much of it off-road to Berney Arms or Burgh Castle. In mid-February I ran the St. Peter's Brewery Great East Run, 20k in a time, (1 hour 17'43"), which was up on the previous two years. Also ran Bury in the midweek league while we were staying at Clare Priory. Richard, Nola and Roy got the train to this one. This was all good so far, but then I went and missed the third Mousehold race in Norwich because I could not be bothered to get up. Not like me at all.

March was Brussels with the students and then the Wymondham Ten in 62'29", (8th out of 140). Mileage was close to 50 miles per week so I felt that I was on the right track. There was cross country twice at Shouldham in the same week - on the Wednesday in the midweek league, (where I lost five places in the run-in to the team from Bury Pacers), and again the following Sunday, when again I did not run well, took the wrong course along with quite a few others, and was beaten by Bert Wilkinson. All in all, I was pleased to see the end of the 2003-2004 cross-country season. At the end of the month I went to Stowmarket for the Joe Cox Ten-miler ,(62'47"), where together with Nola and Mark Turner, I was part of the prize-winning team. Nola was also first lady overall in what turned out to be her last competitive outing to my knowledge before other interests took over. She made such an impression at Stowmarket that I hoped that it would be the springboard to even greater things - but it was not to be. Such a pity.

I had no races in April, but May saw three very useful 10k races at Breckland, (37'54"), 22nd out of 224, Woodbridge, (37'46"), 15th out of 450 and the beating of Phil Quantrill, and Eye, (37'54"), 21st out of 350, where I beat Richard Blake. I was also incorporating track sessions into my training at the time.

June began with the Wroxham 5k race, (18'21"), 27th out of 206, the City of Norwich Half, (1 hour 22'35"), 22nd out of 1000 at a pace of 6'18" per mile over a new, two-lap course; and the Wymondham Midsummer Ten miler, (62'13"), 10th out of 144, where I beat Dale Hurren among others. Things slowed down in July and included a disastrous visit to Dorking with Christopher. The least said about this the better. Then came the Mettingham 10k, (37'41"), where I was the first over 50 and very pleased. All of this was leading to my next marathon, my 35th, at Aarhus in

Denmark where I went with Patrick.

Sunday 1ˢᵗ August 2004   **European Veterans' Marathon, Aarhus, Denmark**
I had thought that my previous marathon, in Amsterdam, had been one too many. This sort of confirmed my suspicions. For some reason I did not really like it. Perhaps because they are becoming too hard. Also I had been building up to it/looking forward to it for so long that it was bound to be an anti-climax. Truth to tell I was rather disappointed with Denmark in general and Aarhus in particular, the former predicated by the excellent family holiday we had there in 1990; the latter by my being quite out of things as far as Patrick was concerned. That said, the arrangement to meet him and fly out of Stansted worked well, if a little expensive. Stansted was a nightmare to get out of as usual, but get out we did and flew into Aarhus, taking a bus into the city. There was a slight hiccup at the hotel, (isn't there always?), as our booking had been cancelled - but we got in eventually. This proved to be something of a mixed blessing as it was the noisiest hotel I have ever stayed in and we got very little sleep the whole time we were there.

Saturday was ok, with registration and so on. Early rising (5am) on Sunday did not really suit me but the 8am race start was great as it never got too warm. I also managed to get myself on the front line. The course was very scenic, (forest, town and lake), with a single loop and not much in the way of hilly sections. The first 10k went to plan, (40'37"), as did the next, (20k in 1 hour 21'41'), and I was at half-way in 1 hour 25'. It was the next 10k which was to prove to be the major problem. I reached 30k in 2 hours 04' so the third 10k had taken me over 42 minutes, very close to the time I was allowing myself. 35k in 2 hours 26' left me 7k to do in 34 minutes. I was not sure at this point if I was going to make it, but rallied in the final 10k, passing the Norwegian third lady amongst others to finish in 2 hours 58 minutes and 17 seconds. This placed me 6th in my age group, slightly higher than I expected. But the time was disappointing and perhaps bears me out about retiring from marathons after Potsdam. As a rather negative postscript, the results service was crap and Patrick let me down rather badly, (I thought), on our last night in Denmark. Oh the foibles of youth! This, incidentally, was to be my 30th and last sub-3 hour clocking

Finishing time : 2 hours 58 minutes 17 seconds
Position : 6th out of 48 in 55-59 age category

The rest of August was gentle running, a delightful Baltic cruise with Mary on the mv Discovery, (mainly treadmill work), and, on our return, the Scores race at Lowestoft, where I was the fourth member of the second team, (23rd out of 170).

September began with a lot of off-road work and then the Grunty

Fen Half Marathon, (1 hour 23'45"), which seemed a lot harder than I remembered it, but where I was 30th out of 572, 2nd over 55 and 1st EVAC over 55. The following Saturday was the Round Norfolk Relay, where I should have run 15.6 miles on the first leg but went wrong twice and actually ran at least 17 miles instead. There was much ribbing and jocularity over this but I was pleased with the outing. It is a privilege to run through such delightful parts of Norfolk as this. Mileages were a little down, (especially Tuesdays and Thursdays, which wasn't good), but the Felixstowe half in October revived my spirits as I ran strongly, (1 hour 22'18"), and beat Mark Turner in the process. There was then Blencathra and cross-country again at RAF Barnham and, the following week, beautiful Bacton where we had a good turn-out in muddy conditions. November was the Ryston 9k, EACCL at UEA and the Norwich cross-country at Mousehold.

The year ended with December races at Bacton once again for cross-country and at Buxton for the Christmas 5k race, where we were chased by horses. An interesting end to an interesting year.

2004 - stats

Total Mileage for year : 2090
Cumulative Mileage : 48009
Number of Marathons : 1
Number of races : 29

2005

I started the year with a race on January 1st. I can't remember if I ever did this before. I ran the Wymondham 10k in 38 minutes 28 seconds which placed me 23rd out of 299, but was quite disappointed with this performance as I struggled a little and did not feel that I did myself justice.

I ran 25 miles in the first three days of year but after that faded a bit as I did not feel so good. So only 37 miles for the week but I did do cross-country at Mousehold Heath on the Sunday in rather icy conditions and with plenty of dog walkers around.

Races 3 and 4 followed in rapid succession, first at Ipswich Chantry Park on the Wednesday where there was a good turn out for a race I did not particularly cherish because of the climbs and the grassland sections; and not much better at Ryston on the Sunday for the county championships, where I put in one of my worst performances ever - obtaining nowt in the County Championships and only 4th in the Ryston series. To make a bad situation worse, a large proportion of the field went the wrong way.

January sort of petered out after that, as, though I was close to 40 miles for most weeks, I was only running on average 4 days a week. I should have had a race on the 2nd February but we couldn't get the minibus to start and take us to Bury, so a few of us went to Fritton, (Neil Sibley, Gary Stanly and others), for an enjoyable run in the woods.

Things were OK about ten days later, however, when I ran in the BMAF cross-country championships in Norwich on the Saturday, (along with Richard Blake, John Bone and John Hills), and at Ryston the following day for the 8k event - neither of them very uplifting but at least I was there at the start line for each event. This was increasingly becoming my main objective.

This busy weekend was followed in quick succession by races in the midweek East Anglian League at Wattisham, where I ran well but my shoe came apart during the race and I walked into a window at the changing venue; and at Bury for the St. Peter's 20k race where for the first time I questioned my long-term future in road races, such was my discomfort (mental and physical) during the race. I was very cold, wearing only a vest and shorts, and would happily have joined anyone in a hut with a fire along the route, but there was no such thing. O for the Marathon du Medoc, (a race I never did), with its regular wine stops offering warmth, solace and bonhomie.

I had a quiet final week in February but did get to Mousehold to complete the third and final race in the Mousehold Cross

Country, (having missed the third race last year), clinching the O55 award in the process. Then March began with Brussels week and no running except 5 miles before leaving and 5 miles upon return. Brussels city centre is not the best place to run, though there are the Botanical Gardens and I did try to get on the treadmills in a fitness centre with some of the students, but all to no avail. I then found it hard to get going in March at all, with just three sessions per week, though I did manage the final EACCL race on the Wednesday and the final Ryston run on the Sunday, (in the latter, I was 3rd in O55 category for the series).

The following Wednesday saw cross-country relays at Barnham Camp near Thetford where the absence of refreshments was diabolical.

Then the end of March, beginning of April saw some good mileage, also seven sessions a week, but this soon degenerated into three-session weeks and rather unspectacular mileages. There was a bit of a lift at the end of April with the Chase the Train race, where I was 3rd to Richard Blake and Andrew Houghton, with 90 runners behind me. I knew this as I was third to the gate before the road and I had known beforehand that there were 93 in the race. Expecting them to rein me in, it never materialised. Shades of that first Hereward Relay. The prize was a let-down though - entry to another race, the Worstead 5, which I might not have been interested in. Still, I was not going to complain to my old mate Terry Quigley, the race director.

The Breckland 10K the following week produced a slowish time, (38'25"), but I was generally pleased with the outcome. Mary had her second hip operation at the beginning of May and events understandably took a low key. Mileage was now in the 35-40 range. There were no more races for the rest of May and all of June. Jenny and Willis, our two top friends from Cayman, arrived at the beginning of July for a week and I did manage the Mutford relays on the 10th, running my 5k leg in 18'36". I thought that I had a good arrangement here - a 5k warm-up before the race and a 5k warm-down afterwards, with the race in the middle giving me a neat 15k overall. I did that for a number of years.

The following Wednesday I ran the 10k in Broome, third clubman home after Phil Quantrill and Richard Blake. I was quite pleased with this outcome and indeed that the following week at the CONAC 10k when again close to Blake and Quantrill, this time much closer to the latter. Even better was the following Friday when I was 27th out of 377 finishers in the Worstead 5 miles, second to Blake but ahead of Phil Quantrill and Raymond Hill. This,incidentally, was the race entry I won in the Chase the Train race earlier in the year.

August began with a cruise of the Norwegian fjords and Iceland with some excellent courses, notably an excellent trail around Alexund in Norway and some track work at Bergen, Olden in Norway and Akureyi in Iceland. Mary was confined to the ship but I would take off and find either a trail or a local running track for a session. Far from the stereotype of an endless progression of one big meal after another, cruises can in fact be a great opportunity to train both onboard and at the various ports-of-call, always assuming that the right choices are made of course. My ideal arrangement was a two-mile deck walk at race pace plus a swim before breakfast in the cabin; then rest and soup and a sandwich for lunch. Then rest and either a session ashore or on the treadmill followed by a weights session. Then you can eat to your heart's content in the evening, so long as it is not too late. This seemed to work a treat.

Once back, I continued to do some useful track work at the Wellesley and all was now ready for this year's marathon (#36) the WMA Marathon at San Sebastian, Spain

I had been a little ambivalent about this one because of the timing at the end of the summer but I asked for the day off and got it. Holiday training had been mixed, to say the least - road, track, trail and treadmill, (on the cruise ship), with rather low pre-race mileages. Still, I never have been a high mileage person and long runs of 20 miles in training have never made sense to me. Save the long ones for the races themselves is what I say.

Hitting your hand with a hammer makes it worse, not better, the next time.

Transport difficulties not withstanding, I made it via Stansted, Biarritz Hendaye, (on the border where change to narrow-gauge railway - the Euskotren - was necessary), and then on to San Sebastian, (or Donastia, to give it its Basque name). My first sight was the magnificent stadium of Real Sociedad with first class / world class adjacent facilities (eg. swimming pools). I was very lucky to get a room at the big Hotel Aneosta right opposite the stadium and therefore the start, had a nice meal and watched the 1500m finals in the stadium in wonderfully balmy conditions. Heavenly.

Next day saw an early start for the race, a bunfight for the microchips and a meeting with some of my fellow Brits and also the Russian Antonov who had won the gold medal to my silver at Potsdam in 2002. He made a point of coming over to see me at the starting line, knew my name and shook my hand. A very nice gesture on his part, (I beat him on this occasion - but he was better when it really mattered).

I got on the front line at the start, (you can do this with about 900 runners - a near enough perfect number for a marathon in my opinion), and ran conservatively to begin with. I know this as for about 10k in the middle of the race, (around the bay which has to be the European equivalent of Copacabana in Rio), I was in a pack of Spanish runners which was being paced. Doing my Benson Masya impersonation, I was pulling ahead and waiting for them to arrive. Cheeky but confidence-building. This may have been my downfall, however, as I remained comfortable at my planned sub - 42 minute 10ks - fine for the first 20k, but a little over at 30k and over schedule at 40k, but not desperately so.

As we approached the stadium for the final time, (there had been several loops), I had another M55 runner with me, a Spaniard, who did not speak, (miserable sod), but we both knew we were at 2:59. I then paid the price for not checking the finishing arrangements. I thought that we would go directly into the stadium, onto the track and finish - but no, we went around the outside before entering the stadium and still having a lap of the track to complete, effectively another 1¾ laps. So a sub 3 hour timing was out, by just 45 seconds - though there were compensations - team silver, (with me sixth and the next two Brits tenth and eleventh - though I never did get a medal for this), behind the Spanish but ahead of the Germans. I was the first Brit home in my age division and I got a great welcome back at the College. Altogether a most uplifting experience.

Time : 3 hours 0 minutes 45 seconds

The rest of the year saw the Lowestoft Scores race in early September, (won my division); the first leg in the Round Norfolk Relay, (enjoyable as I didn't get lost this year); the Felixstowe Half Marathon, (a favourite of mine but quite a long way behind Mark Turner and Richard Blake on this occasion); and then on to the cross country season.

This began in Bacton Woods, (always a delightful start to the season), was interspersed with a rare outing on the roads in the North Norfolk 7, and then continued on to Wattisham in the EACCL, (a difficult old race, this), and the Ryston 9k. I had serious reservations about doing this last race as this was the week that my dear brother Peter died as I held his hand. All so sudden and so unnecessary. A very traumatic moment which haunts me to this day. Peter was buried on 21st November.

The year ended with races at RAF Homington, Felthorpe Woods, the new venue for the Norwich Road Runners series - Mousehold having outlived its usefulness - and at the UEA at Colney where there was a team of fourteen of us in all. Finally, there was the Outney Common Cross Country on Boxing Day, my 30th race of the year - 12th out of 75.

So a very pleasant year for variety and number of races but a sad year personally.

2005 - stats

Total Mileage : 1,949 miles

Cummulative mileage : 49,958 miles

Number of Marathons : 1

Number of Races : 30+

2006

A predictable start to the year with the Norwich cross-country series at Felthorpe Woods, where I was pleased with my performance. Then three races in five days, starting with the midweek league at Chantry Park, Ipswich on the Wednesday, (3 laps of a tricky, grassland course); the County Championships at Earlham Park, where we were third Norfolk team; and the five mile course at Shouldham Warren on the Sunday (third in age group). Then a quiet couple of weeks saw January out - with me averaging 40-plus miles a week.

Some good sessions and weekly mileages continued in February, interspersed with track sessions, some good sessions with Neil and Jeff, meeting Patrick and his Finnish girlfriend, (delightful), in London and managing at trip to Liverpool to boot. The middle of the month saw the eighth race in the midweek league, at Barnham Camp over three laps of a very pleasant woodland course. There was no let up the following Sunday either - with the 9k course at Shouldham where I was first in my age category. Then two more races the following week - EACCL race 9 at Bury, (two laps of a parkland course); and the final race in the Norwich series, which I was pleased with as the previous day I had had to cut my harbour mouth session short because of some chest pains, (25th February 2006). Was this the first sign that I was doing too much?

Had a few days off after this but still managed 40 miles the following week and the final race in the midweek league - 9k at Shouldham Warren completing a very successful season in that league. I was now in a position to tackle my first road race of the season, the Broadland Half Marathon, where I finished 20th out of 260, being generally pleased with the speed at which I ran but not with my overall time, which was my second slowest ever over the distance. So the writing was again on the wall, it appeared.

The following week saw the cross-country relays at Barnham on the Wednesday and the Chase the Train on the Sunday - both of them a little futile but for different reasons. The former because there is little at stake; the latter because of the useless prize of entry into another race, (pace Terry Quigley), even though I was fourth to Richard Blake and two others.

My mileage dipped in early April, including a trip without students to Brussels and a trip to Liverpool, but I was back for the Trowse 10k, 19th out of 263, but my slowest time ever over the distance (39'38"). Things were slightly better two weeks later at the Breckland 10k (39'07") but this was still my third slowest time ever. Mid-May saw me at Dereham for the ten mile race where I was disappointed to finish 23rd out of 200 - behind Andrew

Manning, Neil Sibley and Antony Croucher. This was followed by a dip in training as I had a bad back.

I bounced back however at the end of May in the Great East Anglian Run 10k where I ran my fastest time of the year so far for 10k, (38'48"), and enjoyed the experience as I ran comfortably. There was quite a break then until mid-June and the Wymondham ten mile, not a race I enjoy as it crops up in the middle of the working week. My head was all wrong, (running was perhaps becoming a chore), and I ran one of my worst races ever, though we did get County team gold.

I then ran the Mutford relays in early June, (in one of four teams), and then began to taper for the year's marathon at the end of the month - this time at Poznan in Poland, where six of us headed. Although I was 6th in my age category, the 8 laps around the Malta Lake were not to everybody's liking and my time was my fourth slowest ever, after the first Orange Bowl, Grandfather Mountain and Bolton.

Sunday 30th July 2006   **European Masters Marathon, Poznan, Poland**

Marathon 37, my fourth slowest ever, and perhaps the trigger which I need to make me give them up once and for all. There were positives but also quite a few negatives of a personal and collective nature.

In the party were Neil Sibley, Jeff Helmore, Carole Spong as fellow competitors; Gary Stanley, Jim Spong and Paul Evans as cycling support group. The organisation was a shambles as the organising committee switched from a 2-lap city centre to an 8-lap lakeside course at short notice, mainly because, as is the case in most championship races, (this being the European veteran's marathon), the field was not particularly large and therefore did not, to them at any rate, justify closing off huge swathes of the city centre.

I had not been feeling particularly well in the lead-up to this race, had stopped short in the previous weekend's training with a heart twitch, and so I went to the medicine tent the day before as a precaution, (I didn't tell anyone), and found that my blood pressure was ok (120 / 80) and I was clear to run. Whether this was the right thing to do or not , I just do not know.

The race went OK in the circumstances, (no km markers, no meaningful splits, sheer monotony), and I ran comfortably but with increasing weariness/tiredness due to lack of training over longer distances in the weeks leading up to the race. However I did hold off Neil Sibley, (who does many long runs), and Jeff Helmore, (who was ten minutes behind), so it can't all be bad. So although I was lapped by the leader, I was the first Brit to finish and sixth in my category. Performance of the day, however, was that of Carole Spong, who was second lady F60 and enjoyed her moment of glory on the podium after the race.

I had mixed feelings therefore about this one and the success or otherwise of the event. I enjoyed the group camaraderie but the minibus to the airport was cramped and as for the eight laps of the lake - well, I would probably not have entered in the first place if I had known that this was going to be the case.

Marathon time : 3 hours 12 minutes 10 seconds

The rest of the year went pretty much according to plan, with a gentle August, (though I seemed to be putting on weight), followed by the usual September, beginning with the Wissey Half Marathon, where I was 17th out of 191 finishers and second over 55 but found that, though I nearly beat Pete Johnson in the closing miles, races like these were getting harder and harder. I just seemed to get more and more weary as each race progressed.

The following week saw the Lowestoft Scores, (35th out of 175), always an interesting event, and then the Round Norfolk Relay where I ran the first leg again, finding it rather tough into the headwind and with a considerable degree of dehydration. A ridiculous week followed, including as it did the wedding of my nephew Stephen in Derby, but then we were into October and the cross-country season again - starting with RAF Barnham, where we only made it at the last minute as a result of transport problems. October was also my 60th birthday.

The beginning of November saw my first race as a 60-year old, where I clinched county gold at the Guy Fawkes 10k in Norwich, (39'48"), obtaining a £25 voucher and Grand Prix Number 1 in the process. Then it was back to cross country at Ryston (9k - first over 60), Fritton, (excellent turnout), and Norwich, culminating in a December race at Wattisham, a bout of flu and that was that for the year.

2006 - stats

Total mileage - 2000 miles
Cumulative mileage - 51,958
Number of marathons - 1
Number of races - 28

2007

I took a rest day on New Year's Day, (not a good idea), but then I was straight into things with a 40 -mile week and the first cross-country race of the year at Norwich where I was pleased with my performance. Then Ryston the following week for the County Championships, where I was first over 60, though I lost a shoe and there was a mix-up at the front of the field which meant that they are unlikely to have the championships there too soon again in the near future.

There were some good mileage weeks for the rest of January, but no more races until an interesting first weekend in February when, in company with Jeff Helmore, Martin Pigott, Ian Liffen and Andrew Manning, I was in Ruislip, Middlesex for the South of England Cross Country Championships, (6th out of 60 in my age group) - a very enjoyable outing. I particularly like these Saturday races as they go back to the grass-roots origins of the sport when all of the big cross-country races were held on Saturday afternoons - just like the football matches. Then the following day I was up at Houghton Hall for a pleasant parkland run in a charity race - first over 60 in this, Chris Harbord in attendance.

The following week was the midweek league race at Colney where I struggled - perhaps because I was beginning to feel the effects of the flu which knocked me back later in the week. I even did my first walk to the coastguard at this time. (Walking involves shallower breathing, so you are less likely to get cold air on the lungs). Some new training routes were also introduced - always a good idea to inject new life into your programme. The next race in February was the final Norwich cross-country race - enjoyable, but times seemed to be getting worse by the race.

The final race in February was the Bury midweek race, a very tough run over two laps of a parkland course. I was fifth finisher in our contingent. Two weeks later there was the Shouldham Warren race, which was effectively the last race in the eight-race series.

It was back to the roads at the end of March for the Broadland Half Marathon, where I was first over 60 and 23rd out of 290+, though times continued to depress. They did so two weeks later at Trowse for the 10k, where I was first over 60 but was 30 seconds down on my time of six months previously; and, more alarmingly, went over 40 minutes for the distance for the first time almost in living memory. Chase the Train two weeks later was a bit more low key and I enjoyed the outing and winning my age division.

The Breckland 10k, one of my favourite races over the distance, the following week continued the high and my belief that plenty of short, sharp 10k and five mile races are ideal preparations for the marathon. First over 60, 30th out of 341, and under 40 minutes again - these were all pleasing statistics. I was similarly pleased with the Great East Anglian Run a week later - a similar time, first over 60 but very tired afterwards.

In May I introduced some track sessions and there was some good mileage in June which culminated in the Hethel Engineering Ten Mile Race, where my time was another personal worst, I nearly missed the start, I was only 27th out of 205, and I got into trouble later on for implied adverse comments I made about the prize structure in a letter to Athletics Weekly. Yet, these points notwithstanding, I quite enjoyed the race and always endeavoured to support new events on the road-racing calendar to take place alongside or even replace the rather monotonous and repetitious long-standing events. In the Hethel case, just being at the Lotus headquarters was a treat, with pictures taken underneath one of their most recent models hanging on the wall.

I even did the Wroxham 5k this year, never one of my favourite races because of the sheer intensity of it all. Even so I was first over 60 and got Norfolk gold, so it was well worth the evenings' outing - though my time was another personal worst. Early July then saw the Mutford Relays, (five teams, me in team B), which I enjoyed as usual and won my age division.

Late July brought an appearance in the Worstead 5, (I had won the entry in the Chase the Train race), a Friday evening event the timing of which is not particularly to my liking - but I did win my age division, running comfortably though in a time which was not particularly special, (31'56"). The following day's Fitness Challenge on Gorleston Cliffs was an interesting diversion but hardly justified the resources and effort we had put into it.

In August we were in Liverpool to visit family and to embark on our cruise on the Black Prince to Lisbon, Tangier, Cadiz and Seville. Much work was done on the treadmill and in the pool and occasionally ashore with the Portugese and the Spanish, a great bunch of lads. (I worked out that I did at least a marathon on the treadmill - me and Chris Slavin often working together. Chris is a great veteran runner from Liverpool, still going strong in and winning races in the over 65 category.).

The end of August saw a trip to Paris for our 32nd wedding anniversary where I had a circuit between the Pont de Sully and the Pont D'Austerlitz. Then it was back to work with the enticing prospect of the next marathon, bang in the middle of the month.

Saturday 15th September 2007   **World Masters Marathon, Riccione, Italy**
Marathon 38

This was a nice outing and I wish that during my time with the Great Yarmouth Road Runners there had been more occasions like it. It was up there with the Micky Munt trip to the Great North Run in 1991, the Gateshead jamboree in 1999 and more recent forays to Ruislip for the cross-country.

On this occasion there were four couples, Jeff and Jackie Helmore, Jim and Carole Spong, Ken and Doreen Overy - all of whom arrived early and were nicely ensconced in the excellent Golf pensione/ hotel with its own beach, pool - the lot. Mary and I arrived on the Friday and left on the Sunday, the race being on the Saturday.

Conditions were very hot, despite the early start, for the two-lap course which took in much of the excellent, (and busy), promenade. Jeff Helmore went out fast but I overtook him at the half way mark - though he did recover and I did have him on my mind in the second half. Carole Spong ran her usual measured race but had a bad time of it afterwards as she was very dehydrated and had to spend several hours in the medical tent on a drip being rehydrated afterwards. Despite one or two shambolic elements of the organisation, we all agreed that it had been a trip well worth the taking.

From my viewpoint, (7th in age category out of 80 finishers), I was pleased that I was pretty close to my Poznan time of the previous year, (just 41 seconds slower), and that I did not experience too many difficulties during the race. However, the downsides were the great weariness I felt in the second part of the race, (no Pizzolato-type negative splits here) and the fact that it was now my fourth slowest time ever. However, Mary and I enjoyed the trip immensely, (how did I ever go to those earlier marathons without her?), and I got a good welcome back at the college.

Time : 3 hours 12 minutes 51 seconds

The rest of the year saw the predictable Blencathra trip, a bout of flu and then the cross country season, bang on schedule with races at RAF Barnham, Wattisham ,(mainly on tarmac which I was not happy with), had chest pains the following day followed by river flooding at night, then Broome Heath, Colney, (Ienjoyed this immensely as I only did it after taking advice from Paul Westgate), the Buxton Christmas Fun Run, the Ryston 6.5k and finally the race on Boxing Day at Outney Common near Bungay. Whew!

2007 - stats

Total Mileage - 1922
Cumulative mileage - 53880
Number of marathons - 1
Number of races - 25

2008

A cold and slow start to the year with a run to California and then the question : "Where have all the dunes gone?". Eleven miles on the first Saturday of the year followed by the first Norwich cross-country on the Sunday prompted me to ask if it was not now time to pack it all in. As my log man, Marty Jerome, put it - facing limits is an important life skill.

However, on we went to the midweek league at RAF Barnham, (much more enjoyable than the Sunday race), another one the following week at Fritton and a charity race at Lakenheath at the end of the month - which I was pleased with as there was no pressure and I finished 16th out of 100, winning my age division in a race which I would recommend. I was also training the marathon distance and more over Thursday, Friday, Saturday and Sunday (11.5, 5, 9.5 and 6 miles).

February saw another great trip to Ruislip, with Jeff Helmore, Andrew Manning and Neil Sibley this time, for the South of England Championships where I was 9th out of 47 over 60s and enjoyed the woodland course immensely. The following week, in almost spring-like conditions, there was the fifth race in the Ryston series, this time the 6.5 course where I was first over 60. Chris Harbord also took part here. Two races the following week, at Shouldham in the midweek league, (very pleasing), and then at Wimpole Hall in Cambridgeshire for the EVAC cross country championships - a pleasant run but hard work over the parkland course. Richard Blake won his age division. With two more races the following week, Bury in the midweek league and Norwich on the Sunday, this gave me 6 races in all in February, a pleasing statistic.

March began with the Muddy Marvel at Lode Fen, a marvellous race where I was accompanied by Chris Harbord and won my age division. This was certainly one to recommend. The more conventional season was drawing to a close at RAF Barnham in midweek and then came the advent of the road-running season with the Broadland Half Marathon run in very inclement conditions, with howling wind and rain. Times for the distance continued to regress and this may well have been my last half marathon race, (90'49"). The end of March also saw Patrick off around the world and we were all sad to see him go.

There was a slight resurgence at the very end of this month when Mary and I were at Banbury for the British Masters Cross-Country championships - a great occasion, though it seemed a lot longer than the advertised 8k, (or was I imagining things?) Kevin Youngs was there in his smart car and we also met many of the cognoscenti like Steve James of Southport. Then off to Liverpool via Shrewsbury. April saw the beginnings of preparation for Slovenia with a training double-header on the Saturday and a fastish run on the Sunday. Steady mileage weeks followed but there wetre no races between 29th March and 11th May when I ran the Coltishall Jaguars Spring 5k, pipping Paul Brookshaw in the final mile - though both of us won our age divisions.

Late May saw a trip to the Jazz Festival in Brussels and then back to steady 40-plus weeks in June, ending with the Humpty Dumpty 10k at Reedham, another personal worst but I was second clubman home, to Paul Brookshaw. I was outrun by Martin Yeomans on the run in, however.

I was in Cambridge for training, (work), in late June/early July and the following week did the Mutford Relays, along with 23 others from the club making four teams. I ran two legs and just failed to win my age division, among some controversy. Gorleston-in-Gear was at the end of July, (input-output ratio again disappointing), and then all was ready for the Slovenian marathon.

Sunday 3rd August 2008   **European Veterans' Marathon**
Marathon 39

This was an event and a half for a variety of reasons. Mary and I flew out to Ljubljana on the Friday and were initially very impressed with the city and the café culture, though less so with the hotel, which was rather noisy and not air-conditioned in the rather sultry heat. At registration on Saturday we met Walter Hill, the ultra marathoner - a very pleasant chap - as well as old acquaintances like Bridget Cushen.

The race started early on the Sunday in a sort of penumbre or misty gloom - something I had not encountered in a race before. This soon cleared and the sun started to take its toll. The course wended its way through picturesque villages, farmland and woods - so no problems there - but it was very undulating and the heat was a factor. Indeed I had to walk for some sections of the final third. So although my half-way time was reasonable, (1 hour 34 minutes), and I did rally on the run-in; my time was one of my slowest ever, even though I was 7th in my age division.

Time : 3 hours 17 minutes.

There was quite a postscript to all of this as we were really at the beginning of our Odyssey after the race. After a couple of days in the delightful Ljubljana, we took the train to Zagreb on the Wednesday and the following Friday the overnight train to Split, also in Croatia. What a trip this was in the company of a mad Italian and his family, drinking and singing.

Split was not to our liking, (too crowded, no suitable accommodation), so we took the bus that same day to Medjugordje in Bosnia - Herzegovina where we had a most wonderful time, serendipity meaning that our apartment was right next to the Basilica. What an experience. Then on to Sarajevo via Mostar for two nights in that most exciting city, then overnight train to Zagreb, (in a hotel renamed after the war), and two more nights in Ljubljana before our flight back to Stansted.

Late August saw a trip to Liverpool and then back to routine, with weekly training in the mid-twenties, the Lowestoft Scores Race, always one I enjoyed and this year was no exception, (27th out of 136; 1st over 60). Training was now comfortable but not challenging and I was becoming very depressed. Blencathra was OK, though no Mike Hall on this occasion, and then we were back to the cross-country season, with races at RAF Barnham, (emerging talents), Fritton Lake, (Suffolk league - an excellent single lap course), Ryston, (9k course), Broome (another Suffolk league race over a very pleasant 4-lap course around the lake), Whitlingham Broad, (a new race on the calendar but with only limited participation), the Ryston 6.5k race at Shouldham Warren, (only 3 of us present ; I was first in my age division) - ending the year with our trip to Brussels.

So an interesting year with some telltale signs of deterioration. Summed up, I think, by one little lad whom I encountered on my Berney Arms run one Saturday Morning asking me whether I was walking or running. It really was that close.

2008 - stats

Total Mileage - 1733

Cumulative mileage - 55613

Number of marathons - 1

Number of races - 25

2009

The year started quite well, with five races in January alone, (at Horsford, Colney for the Norfolk Champs, Barnham, Shouldham and Biggleswade - all of them cross-country and all of them very enjoyable). I was managing only four sessions a week, however, (usually Sunday, Tuesday, Thursday and Saturday), and on reflection was beginning to look forward to the days off.

February brought some low mileage weeks and just three races, at Fritton, Bury and the final race in the Horsford series, though run at a very leisurely pace. March then began with a very muddy race on the Stody Estate near Holt, (another Terry Quigley production), with the final East Anglian Cross Country League race at Barnham about ten days later and then mid-month the aptly named Muddy Marvel at Lode Fen in Cambridgeshire - a 160-mile round trip but well worth it. I won my age division. I was also up to five sessions at last.

It was at this point that I was stopped in my tracks when I went to see the dermatologist about the removal of a basal cell carcinoma from my leg and was shocked to discover that I had high blood pressure and my weight had ballooned to 161 lbs. Later that day I had a bit of a panic attack, called out the paramedics and had an ecg - the first of many. March sort of petered out as a result of all this and April saw just five runs in the first half and a big effort to clear out and sell my Aunt's house in Penny Lane, Liverpool - this took quite a lot out of both myself and Mary.

On Friday 17th April I did my first timed walk - 5 miles over the dunes to Caister and back. This was my first mistake in contemplating a switch perhaps to race walking - trying to walk old running routes and going off-road. I have since come to understand that a completely different approach is called for, with new, often shorter, routes over on-road courses with very little in the way of changes in elevation. 5 walks in April became 7 in May, though I was still running also, (13 runs in May so the balance was still in favour of the latter).

It was then June when walks exceeded runs for the first time, (a 14: 2 ratio). This was mainly because I had checked myself into the hospital with chest pains on the 3rd of June, the very day that Paul Brookshaw had died while out running. What a shock this was to so many people. Although I was given the all-clear after spending the whole day in the hospital that I had not had a heart attack, I understood that I would now have to be more careful and since then I have had a series of follow-up tests with the cardiologists at the James Paget Hospital and remain on blood pressure tablets to lower the blood pressure.

I realised at this point that running needed to take a back seat until all was right and with this in mind I felt that walking provided an ideal alternative - not something which could replace running in my affections but a perfectly satisfactory substitute when running was neither possible nor advisable. The rest of June was therefore very quiet, although I did join in the tribute race to Paul Brookshaw at the Wroxham 5k on the 24th of June along with most other members of the club.

July then saw a plethora of walks, (23 in all), including my first walking race, at Newmarket on the 12th, where I walked three miles in 32 minutes and 40 seconds and had a wonderful time at the culmination of the Richard Dunwoody 1000-mile challenge. I also met Ron Wallwork, a stalwart of walking in this part of the country. Though I am never going to be really competitive in race walking, (having taken it up too late), it does afford me a set of new and interesting challenges, quite unlike those of my running career.

In August we then had almost a month back in Cayman with regular morning walks along the aptly-named Walker's Road. Upon our return, I began to consider interspersing walking and running once again - and this seemed to work nicely for the remaining months of the year - though the running side of things remained to the fore. I also managed a very slow initial race in the midweek league at RAF Barnham in October - probably the

lowest I have ever been placed in a race in this league -
followed by Easton and Colney in November, rounding the year
off with a delightful new race at Reepham in December. All told
this gave me 16 races for the year, all of them cross country.
Not a bad haul considering all that had gone before.

2009 - stats

Total mileage   800

Cumulative mileage   56413

Number of marathons   0

Number of races   16

No memory of having starred
Atones for later disregard,
Or keeps the end from being hard
— Robert Frost *Provide, Provide*

MARATHON RECORD

1.	12.01.80	ORANGE BOWL, MIAMI, FLORIDA, USA.	3.31.15
2.	05.04.80	ORANGE COUNTY, LOS ANGELES, CALIFORNIA, USA.	3.09.57
3.	12.07.80	GRANDFATHER MOUNTAIN, BOONE, SOUTH CAROLINA, USA.	3.19.18
4.	17.01.81	ORANGE BOWL, MIAMI, FLORIDA, USA	2.48.15
5.	07.03.81	GALVESTON, TEXAS, USA.	2.52.37
6.	20.04.81	BOSTON, MASSACHUSETTS, USA.	2.47.42
7.	16.01.82	ORANGE BOWL, MIAMI, FLORIDA, USA.	2.48.33
8.	11.07.82	NORTH TYNESIDE, NEWCASTLE, ENGLAND.	2.51.46
9.	22.01.83	ORANGE BOWL, MIAMI, FLORIDA, USA.	2.47.01
10.	24.07.83	BRISTOL, ENGLAND.	2.48.06
11.	21.08.83	BOLTON, ENGLAND.	3.17.10
12.	04.03.84	NEW ORLEANS, LOUISIANA, USA.	2.58.38
13.	30.09.84	MINNEAPOLIS, MINNESOTA, USA.	2.44.08
14.	28.10.84	NEW YORK, NEW YORK, USA.	2.49.45
15.	17.02.85	ORLANDO, FLORIDA, USA.	2.40.56
16.	14.07.85	SANDWELL, WEST BROMWICH, ENGLAND.	2.47.26
17.	13.07.86	GAINSBOROUGH, LINCOLNSHIRE, ENGLAND	2.48.35
18.	26.10.86	CHICAGO, ILLINOIS, USA.	2.52.09
19.	20.02.88	ORANGE BOWL, MIAMI, USA.	DNF
20.	22.04.90	LONDON, ENGLAND.	2.49.56
21.	21.04.91	ROTTERDAM, NETHERLANDS.	2.47.48
22.	15.03.92	BARCELONA, SPAIN.	2.48.56
23.	21.06.92	LIVERPOOL, ENGLAND.	2.48.39
24.	05.06.93	STOCKHOLM, SWEDEN.	2.59.22
25.	24.04.94	PARIS, FRANCE.	2.50.08
26.	23.04.95	TURIN, ITALY.	2.52.45
27.	14.04.96	VIENNA, AUSTRIA.	2.59.10
28.	13.04.97	ANTWERP, BELGIUM.	2.52.26
29.	24.05.98	PRAGUE, CZECH REPUBLIC.	2.51.55
30.	06.09.98	STOKE FERRY, NORFOLK, ENGLAND.	2.50.45
31.	08.08.99	GATESHEAD, ENGLAND.	2.52.40
32.	16.07.00	JYVASKYLA, FINLAND.	2.59.22
33.	25.08.02	POTSDAM, GERMANY.	2.54.17
34.	19.10.03	AMSTERDAM, NETHERLANDS.	2.54.56
35.	01.08.04	AARHUS, DENMARK.	2.58.17
36	03.09.05	SAN SEBASTIAN, SPAIN.	3.00.48
37.	30.07.06	POZNAN, POLAND.	3.12.10
38.	15.09.07	RICCIONE, ITALY.	3.12.51
39.	03.08.08	LJUBLJANA, SLOVENIA	3.17.45

RECORDS

Distance	PB	Races	Achievements	Championships
Marathon	02:40:56	39	30 sub 3 hours	European Silver 2002, Norfolk Champion 1998
Half Marathon	01:15:50	53	24 sub 1:20 hours	Cayman Champion 1985
10 Miles	00:59:18	30	27 sub 1:03 hours	
10 Kilometres	00:35:18	67	52 sub 38 minutes	
5 Miles	00:28:05	18	12 sub 30 minutes	
5 Kilometres	00:16:55	21	17 sub 19 minutes	

(All records are for period from 1st January 1980 to 31st December 2009)

Running community in Cayman referred to in text

Broderick, Michael
Brown, Alexander
Bush, Marlon
Butler, Tim
Byrne, Tim
Davies, Malcolm
Davies, Roger
Elliott, John
Everet, Chris
Flowers, Frank
Ford, Terry
Harper, Jerry
Jobling, Paul
Jones, Alan
Kean, George
Legge, Raymond
Lundie, Chris
Miller, Johnny
Peek, Richard
Ribbins, Pete
Rivers, Greg
Seymour, Curtis
Wessel, Jack
Wilson, Ed
Yeomans, Roger
Rodgers, Bill

Other Cayman

Duggan, Nick
Elliott, Ann
Faranda, Brigid
Faranda, Tommy

Goring, Ferdie
Moore, Benny
Moore, Jenny
Samuels, Esther
Samuels, Ritchie
Sinclair, Charles
Thompson, Allan
Thompson, Hilda
Pashell, Hector

Running community in UK referred to in text

Alder, Jim
Barwick, John
Blake, Richard
Blackwell, Luke
Bone, John
Brightman, Pat
Brookshaw, Paul
Busch, Jorgen
Chester, Gordon
Collins, Mike
Craze, Eddie
Croucher, Antony
Cushen, Bridget
Evans, Paul
Gathercole, Derek
Gooch, Len
Gratton, Mike
Groves, Mike
Harbord, Chris
Helmore, Jeff
Hill, Raymond
Hill, Ron
Hill, Walter

Hills, John

Hogg, Chris

Houghton, Andrew

Hurren, Dale

James, Steve

Johnson, Pete

Jones, Hugh

Kitchener, Brian

Liffen, Ian

Manning, Andrew

Martin, Eamonn

Matthews, Harry

McLeman, Mike

McLeman, Jane

Moore, Matthew

Munt, Micky

Norman, Dick

O'Leary, John

Overy, Ken

Pigott, Martin

Polley, Richard

Powell, Mike

Quantrill, Phil

Quigley, Terry

Ribbands, Derek

Rojmein, Ton

Rudrum, Martyn

Sexton, Bob

Sibley, Neil

Slavin, Chris

Smith, Mike

Spong, Carole

Spong, Jim

Stacey, Martin

Stanley, Gary

Thompson, Angie

Thurtle, Gary
Turner, Mark
Turner, Nola
Turner, Roy
Vaughan, Kevin
Wallwork, Ron
Westgate, Paul
Wilkinson, Bert
Yeomans, Martin
Youngs, Kevin
Zupan, Gary

Other UK

Curran, Johnny
Foster, George
Harton, Eugene
Harton, Rita
Pike, Bryn

Acknowledgements

Thanks go to:

Patrick Spragg for his patience, good humour and expertise in editing the copy.

Christopher Spragg for his unfailing support.

And, above all, Mary Spragg for never failing to support and encourage me in all my endeavours.

Also to all those mentioned in the book who have been such a pleasure, joy and inspiration to run with.

www.ingramcontent.com/pod-product-compliance
Lightning Source LLC
La Vergne TN
LVHW051640080426
835511LV00016B/2408